The Twentieth Century:
A World History

The
New
Oxford
World
History

The Twentieth Century: A World History

R. Keith Schoppa

OXFORD
UNIVERSITY PRESS

OXFORD
UNIVERSITY PRESS

Oxford University Press is a department of the University of Oxford. It furthers the University's objective of excellence in research, scholarship, and education by publishing worldwide. Oxford is a registered trade mark of Oxford University Press in the UK and certain other countries.

Published in the United States of America by Oxford University Press
198 Madison Avenue, New York, NY 10016, United States of America.

Library of Congress Cataloging-in-Publication Data
Names: Schoppa, R. Keith, 1943– author.
Title: The twentieth century : a world history / R. Keith Schoppa.
Description: New York, NY : Oxford University Press, [2021] |
Series: New Oxford World history series | Includes index.
Identifiers: LCCN 2020058375 (print) | LCCN 2020058376 (ebook) |
ISBN 9780190497354 (hardback) | ISBN 9780190497361 (paperback) |
ISBN 9780190497385 (epub) | ISBN 9780197571958
Subjects: LCSH: History, Modern—20th century.
Classification: LCC D421 .S337 2021 (print) | LCC D421 (ebook) | DDC 909.82—dc23
LC record available at https://lccn.loc.gov/2020058375
LC ebook record available at https://lccn.loc.gov/2020058376

DOI: 10.1093/oso/9780190497354.001.0001

1 3 5 7 9 8 6 4 2

Paperback printed by LSC Communications, United States of America
Hardback printed by Bridgeport National Bindery, Inc., United States of America

Frontispiece: The bombing of Nagasaki, August 9, 1945. *World History Archive/Alamy Stock Photo EC80X4*

For you, dear grandchildren, Laurel, Noah, Luke, and Eli—My wish is that you can help transform the spirit of your century—the twenty-first—to bring unity that values diversity, where people, above all, are humane, and where the environment is honored as a harmonious and protected space for productive lives well-lived.

Contents

Editors' Preface

This book is part of the New Oxford World History, an innovative series that offers readers an informed, lively, and up-to-date history of the world and its people that represents a significant change from the "old" world history. Only a few years ago, world history generally amounted to a history of the West—Europe and the United States—with small amounts of information from the rest of the world. Some versions of the old world history drew attention to every part of the world *except* Europe and the United States. Readers of that kind of world history could get the impression that somehow the rest of the world was made up of exotic people who had strange customs and spoke difficult languages. Still another kind of "old" world history presented the story of areas or peoples of the world by focusing primarily on the achievements of great civilizations. One learned of great buildings, influential world religions, and mighty rulers but little of ordinary people or more general economic and social patterns. Interactions among the world's peoples were often told from only one perspective.

This series tells world history differently. First, it is comprehensive, covering all countries and regions of the world and investigating the total human experience—even those of so-called peoples without histories living far from the great civilizations. "New" world historians thus share in common an interest in all of human history, even going back millions of years before there were written human records. A few "new" world histories even extend their focus to the entire universe, a "big history" perspective that dramatically shifts the beginning of the story back to the Big Bang. Some see the "new" global framework of world history today as viewing the world from the vantage point of the moon, as one scholar put it. We agree. But we also want to take a close-up view, analyzing and reconstructing the significant experiences of all of humanity.

This is not to say that everything that has happened everywhere and in all time periods can be recovered or is worth knowing, but that there is much to be gained by considering both the separate and interrelated stories of different societies and cultures. Making these connections is still another crucial ingredient of the "new" world history. It emphasizes connectedness and interactions of all kinds—cultural, economic, political, religious, and social—involving peoples, places, and processes. It makes comparisons and finds similarities. Emphasizing both the comparisons and interactions is critical to developing a global framework that can deepen and broaden historical understanding, whether the focus is on a specific country or region or on the whole world.

The rise of the new world history as a discipline comes at an opportune time. The interest in world history in schools and among the general public is vast. We travel to one another's nations, converse and work with people around the world, and are changed by global events. War and peace affect populations worldwide as do economic conditions and the state of our environment, communications, and health and medicine. The New Oxford World History presents local histories in a global context and gives an overview of world events seen through the eyes of ordinary people. This combination of the local and the global further defines the new world history. Understanding the workings of global and local conditions in the past gives us tools for examining our own world and for envisioning the interconnected future that is in the making.

Bonnie G. Smith
Anand Yang

Introduction

Until 1900, no century in history had known the continually accelerating rate and scope of change experienced in the twentieth century. Its revolutionary discoveries, technological inventions, political realignments, and scientific advances brought radical changes to almost every arena of life. The year 1900 looked very different from 2000. In 1900, there were no antibiotics, few homes with electricity, no airplanes, and very few cars; global life expectancy was about 31 years, and the global literacy rate was less than 30 percent. In contrast, in 2000, global life expectancy grew to 66.4 years—with some countries reaching over 80 years—and the literacy rate soared to 81.9 percent. Though the story of the world in the twentieth century trumpets the triumphs of technology, space exploration, and the miracles of medical science, it is above all the story of men and women, individuals and masses, creating and building, working and playing, scheming and destroying, and constructing and reconstructing their identities through their life experiences. Each individual chose and exuded his or her own identities and were, in turn, accorded identities by others.

An individual has many different identities: biological, spatial, social, political, economic, relational, vocational, habitual, and on and on. Identity can be approached with the question: What defines a person? That is, what values, beliefs, social relationships, and cultural issues are most important to the person? As life moves forward, identities may not be stable; they can shift and change to go along with new experiences, interests, or focal points. One other important consideration is what identities have been ascribed to the person by others and how similar were those attributions. This book focuses on questions of identity with special attention to three personal-political identities that were especially important in the trajectory of the twentieth-century world: the individual and the local, nation-state, and global communities. The range

The Twentieth Century: A World History. Keith Schoppa, Oxford University Press. © Oxford University Press 2021.
DOI: 10.1093/oso/9780190497354.003.0001

of people's identities in specific historical contexts and situations could often produce a clash of identities. Such a clash often became one of the crucial dynamic and motivating factors in historical change. In each chapter, generally five men and women are highlighted; some of them were major historical figures on the world stage, yet the majority were not. Whatever their political, social, and economic status, in the end, all forty individuals from twenty-three countries around the world, who are covered in some detail, acted through their own particular identities to contribute significantly to their world.

A historical vignette from Southwest Africa (specifically, the present state of Namibia) at the beginning of the twentieth century opens this study's focal themes: identity, its meaning, its power, and its roles; violence in various physical and psychological guises; social and cultural change and trends; and the meeting of race, ethnicity, nationalism, and globalization.

They were two very powerful Namibian men, Samuel Maharero of the ethnic Herero tribe and Hendrik Witbooi of the ethnic Nama group. When Maharero first became a paramount chief, even the Herero people found him to be something of a joke: he appeared a spineless and dependent loser. He was a heavy drinker, if not an alcoholic, his rum supplied by the Methodist missionaries before whom he groveled. Witbooi, the paramount chief of the Nama, in contrast, was proudly individualistic and independent, intelligent, well-versed in several languages, and wrote poetry. His people saw him as a charismatic leader and an expert in guerrilla warfare. He raised the ire of the German colonizers by refusing German protection—and what that meant: their domination. When all the other chiefs and paramount chiefs (including Maharero) had given in to the Germans, Witbooi still held out. In his diary, he wrote: "I refused to surrender that which is mine alone, to which I have right; I would not surrender my independence."[1] In the end, he engineered a brief rebellion against the Germans (which he lost), after which he pragmatically capitulated to the Europeans.

Both men became victims of the twentieth century's first gruesome genocide, engineered and executed by the German colonizers in the 1904 to 1907 German-Herero War. Though the word *genocide* was not coined until 1944 (from the Greek *genes*, meaning tribe or race, and *cide*, from the Latin for killing), it has rightfully been used retroactively to describe the Namibian nightmare and the Armenian atrocity a decade later. Here is the story of how the Namibian genocide unfolded.

From roughly 1800 until 1907, Herero and Nama faced each other in almost continual warfare for control of the area. In 1892, their leaders Maharero and Witbooi made peace at last. Ironically, 1892 was also the year that the first German colonizer-settlers arrived to begin farming—though Germany had started the colonization process with missionaries (in the 1840s), trader-merchants (in the early 1880s), and the military (in 1888). When Germany annexed its Southwest Africa colony in 1902, the population was about 200,000, with the native population making up 97.8 percent of the total while the Germans accounted for just 1.3 percent.

The thirty-year experience with imperialistic Germany, from 1885 to 1915, was a nightmare for the Herero. German farmer-settlers needed and wanted two things for their work—land and cattle—and it turned out they were determined to do anything to obtain what they wanted. The Hereros' large territory held some of the colony's best farmland, and they owned the largest herds of cattle—in 1890, an estimated 200,000 head. Indeed, the life and culture of the Herero were focused on cattle. A Herero man's life goal was to increase and preserve his herd. Even more culturally significant, his identity, values, and lifestyle all centered on cattle. The Herero language included over one thousand words to describe markings and colors on cattle.[2] When a baby was named, he or she had to ritually touch the head of a calf, traditionally the ethnic community's birth gift. At a Herero's death, his shroud was made from the skin of his favorite ox, the bleached skull of which was hung on a tree near the grave. Cattle were never killed for food; killing cattle, if it was not on a religious or festive occasion, was sacrilege. In the years 1889 to 1897, a tragic rinderpest (cattle plague) raked over the African continent; it killed hooved animals within days, and some Herero herds lost up to 90 percent of their cattle, ultimately leaving about 90,000 head, a tremendous economic and mythic loss.

From the beginning, the Germans neither understood the culture and actions of the tribesmen nor did they attempt to do so: to the Germans the Herero were simply "black savages," "baboons," "blood-thirsty," and their tribes were castigated as "bands of robbers." The Germans displayed at least two levels of racism. One was an underlying, openly displayed, continuing irritation and downright condemnation of Africans acting as Africans, a bitter, whining "Why-can't-they-be-more-like-us?" A captain on Lieutenant General Lothar von Trotha's military staff complained: "What makes the Herero so revolting is the fact that their way of thinking is completely different from ours. Their logic is not like our logic. How can we communicate with people whose vocabulary does not even contain words such as 'gratefulness,' 'obedience,' 'patriotism' 'loyalty'"? A common German attitude toward the blacks echoed the racist words of General Trotha: "I know the tribes of Africa. . . . They are all alike. They only respond to force. It . . . is my policy to use force with terrorism and even brutality."[3]

The second level of racism was outright physical and psychological abuse—actions that supported the Germans' belief that African tribesmen were not human and, simply put, were worthless. The Germans commandeered one John Cloete, a tribesman in the area (neither Herero nor Nama) to serve as a guide. On their way, they rested at a waterhole. Cloete described what happened.

> While there, a German soldier found a little Herero baby boy about nine months old lying in the bush. . . . The soldiers formed a ring and started throwing the child to one another, catching it as if it were a ball. The child was terrified, hurt, and crying loudly. . . . After a time, they got tired of this and one of the soldiers fixed his bayonet on his rifle and said he would catch the baby. The child was tossed into the air towards him and, as it fell, he caught it and transfixed the body with the bayonet. The child died in a few minutes, and the incident was greeted with roars of laughter by the Germans, who seemed to think it was a great joke. I [Cloete] felt quite ill and turned away in disgust, because, although I knew they had orders to kill all, I thought they would have pity on the child. I decided to go no farther with the Germans.[4]

Psychological abuse clouded most everyday relationships between colonizers and colonials. The German disdain for the tribesmen on the streets, in stores, or in business dealings was shown openly and rudely. For individuals, the German use of flogging, as the major form of "light" punishment, brought both pain and psychological damage. The fact that any German on a whim could flog a black nearly to death without any official approval whatsoever broadcast to the Herero and Nama that their lives were at all times in the hands of the unpredictable whites. Nothing pointed more starkly to the marginalization and powerlessness of the natives than flogging. For the whites, flogging trumpeted their dominance and power. For the blacks, it underscored their racial subordination. It was the whites who decided that the race issue would always be a zero-sum game: "Leniency toward the native is cruelty to whites," said Professor Karl Dove, who served as chair and board member of two German agencies focused on colonialism.[5] Many Germans and other foreigners regarded Dove as the leading authority on Namibia in the last decade of German rule (1905–1914).

As for rampant German disrespect for tribal cultural values and beliefs, two powerful examples suffice; both went to the heart of what the Herero felt was sacred. Both also come from sworn affidavits from Hosea Mungunda, headman of the Herero at Windhoek.

> [We set aside] [o]ur burial places . . . as sacred and holy ground. We selected green trees to build groves [in these graveyards] . . . all those trees were holy and consecrated. No Herero would dare to damage or cut [those] trees. Our two greatest leaders . . . were buried together near Okahandja under beautiful green trees on the river's bank. It was the most sacred place in the whole country [for] all Hereros . . . .
>
> [When] the Germans came, they cut down all the beautiful trees; and turned the sacred burial place into a vegetable garden. They appropriated the place as private property, and no Herero could go there as he would be prosecuted for trespassing. We were terribly upset at this and protested against what we regarded as sacrilege.
>
> Our chiefs complained to the authorities, but no notice was taken.[6]

Mungunda's second example of what can be called "cultural genocide" (actions that obliterated one's cultural heritage and tradition) focused on what the Germans did with the cattle. In the 1890s German farmer-settlers and many merchants began to target Herero cattle; outright German theft and various schemes of granting predatory credit began to thin Herero herds. Since most Herero had little, if any, cash, the merchants and settlers usually demanded repayment of monetary loans *in cattle*. As one arrogant German colonizer put it: "The natives must realize that they cannot have it their way."[7] Governor Theodor Leutwein hit upon a clever scheme to steal cattle. He proposed drawing boundaries (which had never existed) to define clearly the southern "border" of Hereroland. Those cattle that crossed the new unmarked, open boundary were to be impounded; but, instead of returning the cattle to the Herero, the government sold them, with the government and the paramount tribal chief splitting the money.[8]

The German cultural "crime" in these scenarios was that they disregarded completely the Herero tradition of dividing the cattle into "sacred" (or holy) cattle and "secular" cattle. Sacred cattle were inherited patrilineally, from older brother to younger and then from father to son; these cattle were inherited gifts from the ancestors to be passed on to their descendants. Secular cattle, in contrast, were inherited matrilineally from the mother's brother to her sister's son.[9] The sacred cattle's status necessitated that they be retained as a group set apart from all the other cattle.

The Germans obviously had no such categorization as sacred and secular as it applied to cattle. If they stole cattle from the Herero, they could tell no difference between the cattle. With Leutwein's southern border-making, there was no way to know whether sacred or secular cattle crossed the new unmarked border. The Germans had no idea of such a religious-based system, and the Herero would have had no idea that the Germans were unaware of their reality. In his affidavit, Hosea Mungunda first asserted the link between some cattle and sacredness and then argued that the Germans targeting cattle as secular objects was sacrilegious. He said:

> The Germans took sacred cattle and mixed them with private cattle, quite regardless of our customs and organization. We protested and complained bitterly, but the Germans took no notice. Sometimes we persuaded them to return our holy cattle, but then we had to give them three or four ordinary cattle in exchange . . . it greatlydiminished our stock.[10]

This policy had at least two unfortunate, if not calamitous, cultural impacts on the Herero. First, the boundary, in essence, changed the Hereros' spatial world, giving it a new sense of boundedness and therefore a new, less expansive identity. For the wealthiest tribe in the area, this sense of geographical and psychological downsizing was difficult to tolerate. Second, Leutwein's scheme became the mechanism by which more and more cattle disappeared; this process shattered the link that tied many Herero to their ancestors and thus wiped out a chief cornerstone of their cultural traditions.

The issue of land was crucial for German colonizers—even more so than the numbers of cattle. According to local ethnic customs, land was held in common: *no one* could purchase this land. Ethnic community members could sell the "use" of a tract of land but not the land itself. Germans scoffed at such a longtime conception of property ownership and simply, in no uncertain terms, demanded that land be turned over to them. By 1885, Nama tribal chiefs had sold on German demand the Atlantic coastal region from the Orange River in the south to the Kunene River in the north (the borders of present-day Namibia). From the beginning, the Germans perpetrated land fraud on ethnic leaders. The treaties specified that the German-controlled land would extend twenty miles inland from the coast; the ethnic leaders, who had had some experience with the British before the Germans came, took that as being in English miles, which was about 1.5 kilometers. The total distance inland from the coast, tribal leaders figured, was to be about 30 kilometers. However, the Germans used the now-obsolete "geographical" or "German" mile, which was pegged at 7.4 kilometers. Under the German calculations, 20 miles equaled 148 kilometers, or about 91 miles.[11] Through German sleight of hand, the Nama in this case unknowingly gave up a lion's share of their land.

When Africans sought legal protection from German land seizures, they were met by uncooperative, do-nothing officials, whereas the German government quickly sanctioned any settler action no matter what it was. Thus, for the Africans, there was no recourse if they were wronged. There was little objective law as practiced: law was what the Germans said it was. Since there were no established courts in the colony until 1903, the police chief was the one and only judicial administrator: he arrested people, served as jailer, and then as judge. Sentences were handed down on the basis of race. Natives who committed murder invariably received the death penalty; Germans who killed a native were sometimes acquitted, sometimes got several months, or at most (and rarely) received a three- to five-year sentence.[12]

Small rebellious incidents invariably led to more seizures of land and cattle, but for the Herero the largest and most serious theft was their identity. An imperial ordinance in April 1898 established "native reserves," small tracts of land both for keeping natives hemmed in and to facilitate their surveillance. The Germans seized land so the farmer-settlers would have it to farm; but, just as important, they took possession "to deny black Namibians access to the same land, thereby denying them [entry] to commercial agricultural production and forcing them into wage [labor]."[13] The goal: completely overturning the identity and culture of the Herero by making a wealthy people impoverished and making independent and self-directed people totally dependent on servitude to foreign farmer-settlers.

Native ethnic groups also lost traditional lands through the construction of railroads in the region. In the two railroad lines constructed in northern Namibia, farming was not allowed 12.4 miles on either side of the tracks. One of the lines directly struck the Hereros' livelihood. The railroad tracks ran 235 miles through the heart of Herero farmland, taking a 25-mile strip of excellent farmland that they could no longer cultivate. In addition, all the water rights in that strip went to the railroad. The construction of this railroad line was the catalyst for a Herero rebellion from January to August 1904: the railroad project took 27 percent of all Herero land—3.5 million hectares out of a total of 13 million hectares.[14] The Nama followed up with their own insurrection from October 1904 to November 1905. Both insurrections were put down by German armies, and, in the end, the wars provided Germans the pretext for seizing all the land in the colony.

In the German-Herero War, victory in the initial battles went to the Herero, but German firepower rapidly stopped that winning streak. While Governor Leutwein expressed his hope that the warfare could be ended through negotiations, Berlin lambasted that line as too lenient. He was replaced in June 1904 with Lothar von Trotha, a belligerent racist. His obsessive goal was not to simply defeat the Herero but literally wipe them off the face of the earth. He saw the struggle as a "race war, aimed not at the surrender of the Herero but at the destruction of the social core of their existence."[15] He categorically refused any negotiations with the Herero and ordered that his troops never take male prisoners.

Trotha had a genocidal strategy of three different methods to accomplish his goal of killing all the Herero. The first strategy was military extermination. Germany was indeed the victor at the decisive battle of the war (August 11, 1904). But not all the Herero were killed, and several thousand of their troops were not defeated. The second strategy was to drive the remaining Herero deep into the desert, where they would starve or, more likely, die of thirst. Many did. Written in 1909, the official Foreign Office's succinct analysis of the action stated that the war against the Herero, conducted by General Trotha, was one of extermination; hundreds—men, women, and children—were driven into desert country, where death from thirst was their end.[16]

From June through September, it generally does not rain in the Omaheke Desert, and there is very little rain until January. The temperature rises in September to 86°F on average, in October to 91°F, and in November to 92°F. Months of no rain followed by months of extreme heat brought tens of thousands of the marooned Herero to their deaths. Yet Trotha apparently felt no empathy or sympathy for the Herero. He reported on September 13, 1904, that Herero women and children came in large numbers to ask for water, and Trotha gave immediate orders to chase them back by force.

Where possible, the German army blocked water holes so that the Herero could not drink from them. They also poisoned the water holes as they progressed into the desert; any Herero trying to return would find no drinkable water. The rationale from the kaiser via the Imperial Colonial Office: "[We must] thoroughly poison their water supply. After all, we are not fighting against an enemy respecting the rules of fairness, but against savages."[17] On October 2, Trotha issued his infamous extermination orders: "The Herero people will have to leave the country. If the people refuse, I will force them with cannons to do so. Within the German boundaries, every Herero . . . will be shot. I won't accommodate women and children anymore. . . . I shall give the orders to shoot . . . them."[18]

The final solution for those still alive was to send them to notorious concentration and death camps marked by intolerably brutal conditions; historians have seen them, rightly or not, as the likely models for the Nazi death camps established three decades later. In Namibia, two were in the northern interior—at Windhoek, the capital, and at Okahandja, built by the Herero, who made it their main base. The Windhoek camp had five thousand prisoners for whom the daily food allowance was a handful of uncooked rice, with some salt and water. But the two coastal camps in ports on the Atlantic Ocean were far worse in the extent of prison labor, lack of supplies and medical care, and the cruelty and brutality of overseers and guards. At the port of Swakopmund, for example, from February to May 1905, no fewer than 40 percent of the prisoners died.

But the worst fate was for those sent to Luderitz in the far southwest corner of the country, where 80 percent of the prisoners died. An eyewitness account illustrates the realities of the death camp located on the small Shark Island in the harbor. The writer was Samuel Kariko, a Herero schoolmaster who was a son of Daniel Kariko, an important Herero under-chief:

> I went to . . . my old home, and surrendered. We then had no cattle left, and more than three-quarters of our people had perished. . . . There were only a few thousands of us left, and we were walking skeletons, with no flesh, only skin and bones. . . . I was sent down with others . . . to Luderitz [where] there were thousands of Herero and Hottentot [Nama] prisoners. We had to live there. Men, women, and children were all huddled together. We had no proper clothing, no blankets, and the night air on the sea was bitterly cold. The wet sea fogs drenched us and made our teeth chatter. The people died there like flies that had been poisoned. . . . No day passed without many deaths.[19]

In this first genocide in the twentieth century, 81 percent of the Herero were killed in battle, in the desert, and in death camps. In two of the other larger ethnic communities, population losses totaled 51 percent and 57 percent. The total number of natives killed just in these three localized ethnic holocausts was over 92,000. And in a fiendishly sadistic and vengeful knock-out blow to traditional Herero identity and culture, the Germans forbade the Herero to own any cattle or land in the future.

Of the three-tiered identities—local, national, and global—the local is most common here, especially for the Herero who had neither a national nor a global identity but a shared identity with their ethnic group. They also had regional linkages with South Africa. Germans were obviously eager to identify with their relatively new nation-state (established in 1871) and carry its goals forward. A latecomer to colonization, Germany wanted to be seen as a global force among other colonizers: German conduct, then, in Southwest Africa was important for its image (identity) in the eyes of the global community. That was why the kaiser stepped in to end the Trotha genocide.

The overarching storyline in the history of the Herero tribe and Germany's Southwest African colony was how, in imperialist mode, Germany went about destroying the Hereros' identity. Generally, identity changes incrementally over time. The Germans first set out to detract from and then destroy the traditional powerful identity of the Herero and Nama chiefs and paramount chiefs, defeating most in battle. Then through manipulation, trickery, and downright criminal activity, they took the Hereros' and Namas' sources of livelihood, without which their traditional identities were gutted. Through the pressures of that process, they created a "new more white-appropriate identity" for ethnic Namibian groups: their sole role was to be servants to white Europeans "without recourse to legal rights," unable to support themselves either by pasturing cattle or farming, subject at any time to German euphemistic "parental chastisement" via flogging, and paid a meagerly inadequate wage.

Of the three personal political identities, perhaps most important was the individual whose locality served as a focal point in the late eighteenth-century Enlightenment. This focus exalted positive aspects of individualism, defined as "the habit or principle of being independent and self-reliant" and also as "freedom of action for individuals over collective or state control."[20] Clearly Hendrik Witbooi and Lothar von Trotha filled that bill. The premise of individualism is that the individual's interests are or ought to be ethically paramount over others in society and that individuals best serve the public interest by following their own interests. This was the guiding German outlook: they could individually determine their relationship with their subordinate Herero, whether and how to steal his cattle, when to have him flogged, and how far to drive him into the desert. For the Herero and Nama, individualism, apart from Witbooi's earlier willfulness, only brought unwanted attention to the eyes of the enemy; thus, for society's subordinate, individualism was probably not the game to play. Individualism, unchecked, could have a pernicious effect on society and nation by threatening and eroding the cohesion and harmony of families, groups, and the nation-state. Individualism could create great tensions and affect in complex ways the relationship between the individual and the state and the individual or any other individual. An individual's identification with a particular race or ethnicity or with certain goals and outlooks was potentially a fertile soil for germinating conflict between indigenous groups and Germans.

A second significant twentieth-century identity was the nation—the political-social-cultural unit through which humans saw and understood their roles in society and the world and the territorial unit that they identified as their native land. Nation-states have not always been the standard territorial-political unit; before the sixteenth and seventeenth centuries, there had been city-states, dynastic states, tribal states, and multiethnic empires. But by the nineteenth and twentieth centuries, the nation-state manifested itself as the basic political-geographic unit, emerging everywhere around the globe. Nationalism, like local power bases, was also a potential negative force; nations often became provocateurs of international tensions and fears and the main instigators of and combatants in wars. Nations frequently acted like self-interested bullies, belittling other nations, and taking advantage of opportunities to risk their people's lives for money, power, and bragging rights.

The other territorial "unit" that increasingly flourished was the global. Globalization developed under the empires of various Western Europeans in the seventeenth and eighteenth centuries and in the growing world network of trade and interchange in the nineteenth century. Partly from heightened literacy in the world and partly from the communication and transportation revolutions, in the twentieth century, people's contextual awareness increased: they understood more fully how their lives fit in (or did not fit in) with society, with the presence and actions of the other, and with aspects of globalization.[21]

Beginning in the late twentieth century, Gro Harlem Brundtland served as prime minister of Norway (1981, 1986–89, 1990–96), head of the UN's World Commission for Environment and Development, director-general of the World Health Organization (WHO), and UN special envoy for climate change. She spoke about the centrality of globalization for the present and future. "If globalization is to realize its potential as a force for good, we have to look more closely at the means by which we handle our growing interdependence. We do not have a world government, but we do have an increasingly complex network of institutions that are concerned with global governance. They are central to our future and international human rights law."[22]

In the early twenty-first century, there seems an ebb and flow among these three political loyalties, with each territorial level vying for greater control and power vis à vis the others. Was this a reflection of what the world experienced in the twentieth century? Or were the experiences of the twentieth century a mere prelude or period of preparation for what may be a central theme and structure for crucial developments in the twenty-first century? In the end, what roles did the twentieth century play that were most important in setting the twenty-first century on the paths it would follow?

CHAPTER I

The Great War and Social Change, 1900–1919

The more than fifty million people who visited the 1900 Paris World's Fair arrived on foot or in horse-drawn buggies. But like the Time Traveler in H. G. Wells's 1895 novel *The Time Machine*, they entered an unforeseen universe of X-ray machines, wireless telegraphy, sound-synchronized movies, diesel engines, and huge electrical generators. These dynamos powered the breathtaking Palace of Electricity, with its five thousand multicolored incandescent lamps and eight massive searchlights. Visitors rode a two-mile moving walkway (with three speeds) and escalators. An American historian, Henry Adams, overwhelmed by this technology, wrote that "his historical neck [was] broken by the sudden irruption of forces totally new."[1]

For the rapidly industrializing peoples of Western and Central Europe and the United States, the opening years of the century brought both the exhilaration of the scientific and technological revolution and fears of the uncharted realities into which they were being led. Some were particularly apprehensive that new technological forces might alter life patterns and assumptions. As Adams recognized, the values of modern culture could challenge traditional moral values and the social and cultural guideposts that had shaped life's direction. As for the masses, the most immediately useful inventions were the wireless, cinema, gramophone, and the internal combustion engine. But the era's most momentous long-range scientific discoveries did not resonate until mid-century: the detection of the electron (1897), the development of quantum theory (1900), and the theory of relativity (1905).

Over the preceding six decades, northwestern European nations had led the march into industrialization, creating global empires from which they imported raw materials and to which they exported and merchandised finished products. In the midst of technological and demographic changes, society and politics in industrializing Europe were

The Twentieth Century: A World History. Keith Schoppa, Oxford University Press. © Oxford University Press 2021.
DOI: 10.1093/oso/9780190497354.003.0002

The moving sidewalk was a highlight of the 1900 World's Fair in Paris. It ran a 3.5-kilometer circle using two parallel moving platforms: one running at full speed (8 kilometers per hour), the other at half speed. Brown Digital Repository, Brown University Library

also rapidly changing. As peasants from rural society flooded the cities, those centers of industrialization generated an increasingly demanding laboring class. At the same time, the landed elites in the countryside were anxious and uncertain about their future. North America achieved rapid industrialization, but exports were still mainly agrarian products and raw materials. Asia, Latin America, Africa, and Oceania were almost exclusively agrarian, but they did export a range of animal, agricultural, and raw mineral materials: natural rubber, raw sugar cane, coconut and palm oils, guano, seal oil and leather, salt, tea, rice, wheat, cotton, and flax, to name a few. Trade was tying the world's regions together through "globalization," with increasing economic interdependencies and growing political interconnections, leading, in turn, to broadening cultural exchanges. Studies have shown that for the main imperialist powers in their global roles (France, Germany, the Netherlands, the United Kingdom, Spain, and the Unites States) from 1870 to 1913, merchandise exports became a greater and greater share of their economies (as percentage of GDP).[2] This was a clear indication that economically advanced countries were selling modern products manufactured starting in the Industrial Revolution and making the world a global marketplace. The period of globalization from 1870 to World War I might be called the first age of globalization in the modern world.

The vast population migrations in the period from 1860 to 1914 also underscored the march of globalization. Most migrants enjoyed relatively free mobility when crossing borders, in part because of the lack of overbearing state regulations. Decisions to migrate resulted from multiple hopes: for land and higher incomes; for political, religious, or social control of their lives; and for the opportunity to gain freedom from conscription, taxation, or a claustrophobic social system. Labor markets were a major lure. The transatlantic migration was mammoth: 52 million emigrants left Europe for the Americas with 72 percent (37 million) heading to North America and 21 percent (11 million) to South America. Persecution—as in the Russian state pogroms against the Jews—was a potent force prompting migration; between 1899 and 1914, 1.5 million Russian and Polish Jews fled to the United States.

Attendees at the World's Fair could also see some of the 1900 Olympic Games, held concurrently with the Fair. The roster of participating Olympic nations in 1900 suggested a different world reality from the 1896 Games in Athens. In Greece, 85.7 percent of the participants were European, but in 1900, only 58 percent were Europeans. The Eurocentric vision of the world was very slowly beginning to change. Instead, the early twentieth-century global reality placed Western imperialistic globalists in charge of empires made up of their colonies. In the 1900 Olympics two participating units were colonies: India (Great Britain) and Cuba (briefly, the United States). The Netherlands and France highlighted their colonies in national pavilions. The first displayed a model of a Buddhist temple from the Dutch East Indies (today's Indonesia). France exhibited "human zoos" of natives in dioramas simulating the natural surroundings of its African colonies. Racist imperialism was the context for their depiction of the natives: primitive, inferior, exotic, and learning obediently what the whites had to teach.

One of the most challenging tensions at the individual level was the rising visibility and demands of women, who were allowed to participate in the Games for the first time. Their emerging condition, by and large, reflected economic changes: in some Western European countries, they had gained the right to own property and to earn and keep their wages (though they were about half what men earned). Women in large numbers were able to get an education; many non-Catholic countries legalized divorce; laws were enacted to "limit" wife-beating. Some men resented the growth of women's power, seeing it as implicitly questioning their male dominance; in their views, women's suffrage boded nothing less than the death knell of civilization.

In the inauguration of women's suffrage, New Zealand led the way in 1893, Finland adopted it in 1906, and Norway in stages between 1907 and 1913. For perspective's sake, universal manhood suffrage was also not widespread. Norway, Spain, Belgium, Finland, Austria, Sweden, and Portugal had attained it by 1910. But in the century's first decade, it was women's rights organizations that sponsored meetings and rallies to clamor for the right to vote. Women's Sunday, June 21, 1908, drew an estimated 250,000 men and women to a rally in London's Hyde Park, and three of the five speakers were men: George Bernard Shaw; Kier Hardy, a Scottish trade unionist and politician; and Israel Zangwill, a popular author and a leading Jewish Zionist. For their part, demonstrators called upon the government to grant women's suffrage immediately. But Prime Minister Asquith refused to allow the introduction of a suffrage bill. Suffragette protests, including smashing windows at 10 Downing Street, produced ridiculously excessive police reactions: they beat women, punched them, threw them to the ground, and sexually abused them. To answer to the question, "Why women's suffrage?" the suffragette leader Emmeline Pankhurst responded: "We have to free half the human race, the women, so that they can help to free the other half."[3] World War I, however, temporarily silenced the suffragette movement.

The career of Polish-born Marie Sklodowska underscored the predicament of many women in the early twentieth century. Despite her brilliance in chemistry and physics, Polish law forbade women to enroll in universities. In 1891, she made it to Paris, where she earned a physics degree from the Sorbonne. Her desire to return to Poland to teach was thwarted when Krakow University refused to hire her because of her gender. Physicist Pierre Curie, whom she married, convinced her to pursue her PhD in Paris. Collaborating closely with Pierre, Marie developed the theory of radioactivity and discovered the elements of polonium and radium. In 1903, the Royal Institution invited the Curies to London, where Pierre spoke about their research; Marie's gender precluded her from speaking.

That same year the Nobel Prize in Physics was awarded to Henri Becquerel and Pierre, who had first discovered uranium rays, but not to Marie. Pierre's protest compelled the Nobel committee to include Marie in the prize. On April 20, 1995, French President Francois Mitterand led a solemn ceremony in the reburial of Pierre and Marie from a cemetery near Paris to new graves under the dome of the Pantheon.

The purpose, in Mitterand's words: "To finally respect the equality of women and men before the law and in reality."[4] Becquerel received half the prize, and the Curies each a quarter; all three were noted for their work in radioactivity. After a tragic road accident killed Pierre in 1906, Marie continued their work. She became the first female professor at the Sorbonne, a historical breakthrough at the university founded in 1257. She received a second Nobel Prize (for Chemistry) in 1911. For all her brilliance, as a woman she faced repeated barriers in both her native Poland and in France—with the same kinds of attitudes also reflected in England and Norway. Her own attitude revealed her lifetime difficulties: "In 1906, just as we were definitely giving up the old shed laboratory where we had been so happy, there came the dreadful catastrophe which took my husband away from me and left me alone to bring up our children and, at the same time, to continue our work in research."[5]

Another woman sensed early in the century that she had to commit to constitutionalism as a new form of government for China. She was Cixi, the Manchu empress dowager, who had ruled China since 1861 through an authoritarian monarchy. Reformers and revolutionaries had called for constitutional reforms; Cixi believed that she and the government, for the sake of the dynasty's future, had to lead the way in dramatic fashion. Cixi announced a reform calendar to accomplish a specific constitutional step each year on the way to establishing the constitution in 1917.

Although she died in 1908 and the dynasty was overthrown in 1912, her attempt at major political reforms was quite shocking. If gender was a problem for Curie, it was an even greater obstacle for Cixi. Chinese culture was thoroughly patriarchal: throughout life, women were always subordinate to men, whether father, husband, or son. Deeply conscious of her identity as a woman, Cixi had never dared sit on the throne in the Forbidden City's Hall of Supreme Harmony, where the emperor sat. As a proverb put it: "The hen does not herald the coming of morning"— that is the rooster's job. Her taking that throne would have been a claim to total authority and a step that would have been anathema to Chinese men and culture. In essence, however, Cixi transformed herself into a man, ruling for almost half a century as emperor in all but name and mastering the brutal slash-and-burn of court politics. In her years as reformer, Cixi seemed to have become something of a feminist, financially supporting the feminist journal *Beijing Women's News*.

Cixi's gender was a liability in Chinese culture, and her ethnicity was an even more crucial issue. Indeed, many of the most horrific and

The Empress Dowager Cixi hired Xunling, a young Manchu who had studied photography in Paris, to take a series of photographs as a vehicle by which she, following the bloody Boxer Rebellion, could present to the world a more sophisticated and humane image. Xunling, in turn, wanted Cixi to appear to Westerners in comfortable homey contexts—usually surrounded by platters of apples and oranges, arranged in pyramids. Freer Gallery of Art and Arthur M. Sackler Gallery Archives Purchase, 1966. Xunling, FSA A.13 SC-GR-251 catastrophic episodes in the twentieth century rose over ethnic issues, that is, between groups with differing cultural, racial, or religious traditions. In the Chinese revolution, the ethnic struggle was between Manchu and Chinese. Via a bloody conquest in 1644, the Manchus had seized power over the ethnic Han Chinese; yet the Chinese outnumbered the Manchus about 100 to 1. The Manchus thus had to work with the Chinese as they struggled to maintain their own ethnic identity. In the first decade of the century, ethnic tensions became virulently politicized over who was to blame for China's wretched plight in the world—the minority Manchus or the overwhelmingly majority Chinese. Many Chinese suspected that Cixi's championing of constitutionalism was just a Manchu ploy to retain power.

In 1907 a young Han Chinese revolutionary named Xu assassinated a Manchu governor who had strongly supported Xu obtaining an official government position. Xu was seized and executed. His pre-execution statement underscored the strength of Han ethnic hatred: "The Manchus have enslaved us Han. . . . You say that the governor . . . treated me well. Yes, [he did, but that was] . . . the private kindness of an individual person. My killing of the governor, however, expressed the universal principle of anti-Manchuism."[6] Xu's rationale prefigured the thinking of early twenty-first-century assassins because they were not personally aggrieved by the people they killed but more by the "universal principle" of whatever person, creed, or body of ideas they espoused. The culmination of that hatred came in 1911–1912 when the Han, in revolution, overthrew the Manchus.

A second ethnic tragedy in the early twentieth century was the "ethnic cleansing"—that is, genocide—of over one million ethnic Armenians from 1915 to 1917 by the Ottoman Turks. After fighting began for World War I, colonial empires also became arenas for war. Global civilization had transmuted into global war in central Asia. The Turks used the spurious rationale of national security during the war to move Armenians away from the Russian border, in part because of a perceived Armenian sense of Christian congruity with Russian Christians, both of whom theoretically opposed the Turkish Muslims. Because Armenians from all over Turkey were subjected to the genocide, the national security rationale made little sense. But the Turks disparaged the Armenians, belittling their state contributions, their ordinary citizenship, and their lives as primitive and worthless. In reality, the Turks conducted wholesale massacres of healthy Armenian adult males and the mass deportation of women, children, the elderly, and the sick into Middle Eastern deserts without provisions. Marchers were frequently stripped naked and forced to march under the scorching sun until they dropped dead; people who stopped to rest were shot. The Turks thus took a page from General Trotha's "desert strategy" against the Herero. In 1914 there were 2.1 million Armenians; in 1922, there remained only 387,800.[7] In their genocide, the Turks had wiped out about 82 percent of Armenians (1,745,390 Armenians dead). Their almost blasé attitude about killing vast numbers of people was reported by Henry Morgenthau Sr., the US ambassador to Turkey: "When the Turkish authorities gave the orders for these deportations, they were merely giving a death warrant to a whole race; they understood this well and, in their conversations with me, they made no particular attempt to conceal the fact."[8]

In many countries, national reforms occurred through progressive social legislation, rather than through the violence of revolution or genocide. Laws providing for health, unemployment, accident, and old-age insurance passed in Germany in the 1880s and in New Zealand in the 1890s. Australia had the first Labor-majority government in the world from 1910 to 1913, enacting an array of social legislation. From 1900 to 1910, Great Britain installed state-managed and partially financed social security through compulsory insurance; minimum wage laws; progressive taxation; compulsory, free public education; and unemployment coverage. Labor union membership skyrocketed from 1900 to 1914, soaring from 2 to 4 million in Britain, 1 to 3 million in Germany, and 250,000 to 1 million in France. Progressive leadership in Italy and Greece supported organized labor and its right to strike.

The experience of Rodrigues Alves, president of Brazil from 1902 to 1906, revealed how progressive change could spawn violence. Alves served three terms as governor of São Paulo, then Brazil's second-largest city, where he became known as a progressive reformer. As president, he turned his attention to Rio de Janeiro as a first step in modernizing the nation. Rio was known at the time for its swamps, slums, unpaved streets, and epidemics of yellow fever and smallpox. Alves, as city planner, first set out to restructure the city: tearing down city slums, relocating the residents at the city's edges, building and widening newly paved streets, and installing gas streetlamps. Criticism over his readiness to spend government money for such changes turned into unrest when Alves tried to safeguard the health of city residents against epidemics. Quelling mosquito-spread yellow fever was successful by 1906. Reining in smallpox was another matter. Rio recorded almost seven thousand cases in 1904; the only weapon was compulsory vaccination. Because people did not come forward, stiff laws put teeth into

n certificates were necessary for school en-
for travel.

ulations, street rioting erupted in November
ith the reforms' expenses attacked police
on the presidential palace. When military
forces were called on to suppress the insurrection, Military Academy
cadets supported the rioters. Five days later, loyal troops marched
against the Military Academy and put down the insurrection. After this
violent outburst, vaccinations proceeded; within a year smallpox was
under control. Under Alves, Rio was "remodeled," becoming a proto-
type for Sao Paulo and other cities.

In the Balkans, ethnicity was the currency of daily life. Although
Croats, Serbs, Slovenes, and Bosnians spoke Serbo-Croatian, Slovenes
and Croats wrote in the Roman alphabet while Bosnians and Serbs used
Cyrillic. Croats and Slovenes adhered to Roman Catholicism, while the
Serbs and Bosnians followed Eastern Orthodox Catholicism. Although
these ethnicities can be separated for comparison's sake, some scholars
have argued that there were few actual stark delineations among the
ethnicities and that, when it came to the nub of ethnicity, everyone was
polyglot and hybrid. *[handwritten margin note: everyone is from everywhere]* The period 1908 to 1914 saw several military
crises with major players left dissatisfied: Austria annexed Bosnia out-
right in 1908 but was upset by continuing Balkan opposition; Russia
saw the Serbs as Slavic brothers and were angry over the annexation of
Bosnia; and Serbia was embittered by the Hapsburg's repressing its national ambitions to form a Balkan state.

A Bosnian Serb, Gavrilo Princip, the son of a poor farmer, was a
bright and politically driven young man. At the age of fifteen, about
1909, he joined Young Bosnia, a secret society whose goal was to sever

[handwritten margin note: it had never been so easy to stay alive but it had also never been so easy to kill]

s and unite it with Serbia. At age eighteen,
Black Hand, a Serbian nationalist group.
up of conspirators, including Princip, in
z Ferdinand, heir to the Hapsburg throne,
n June 28, 1914. The episode underscores
istory. The seven potential assassins were
the motorcade; the second threw a bomb
ke's car and exploded near a car behind it.
At the sound of the explosion, the motorcade sped up, so that the remaining potential assassins, including Princip, could not fire any shots
or throw any bombs. On its return route, the first two cars in the motorcade turned onto the wrong street, where, it happened, Princip was
standing. When the drivers realized they had made a wrong turn, they

tried to back up, but the archduke's car stalled. Princip walked to within five feet of the car and shot Franz Ferdinand and his wife to death. Too young to be subject to the death penalty, he was sentenced to twenty years in prison, where he died of skeletal tuberculosis. His act was not the cause, but the catalyst for World War I—the "Great War."

The assassination would not have had such impact had the nations of Europe and West Asia not been aligned in two jittery rival camps: the Allied powers—France, Britain, and Russia—and the Central powers, consisting of Germany, Austro-Hungary, and the Ottoman Empire. The assassination set off a chain reaction: in a single week, July 28 to August 4, Austria declared war on Serbia; Russia mobilized in friendship with the Serbs; Germany, unnerved by Russia's mobilization but believing it would win any war, declared war on Russia and then attacked France, trampling its way through neutral Belgium; and for that action against Belgium, Britain declared war on Germany. National rivalries and ambitions fueled the headlong descent into war.

Wilfred Owen recounted in his sonnet "1914" the bleak impacts of the war:

> War broke; and now the Winter of the world
> With perishing great darkness closes in . . .
> Is over all the width of Europe whirled.
> Rending the sails of progress. Rent or furled
> Are all Art's ensigns. Verse wails. Now begin
> Famines of thought and feeling.
> Love's wine's thin.
> The grain of human Autumn rots, down-hurled.[9]

After the fighting began, colonial empires also became arenas for war. Global civilization had spread into global war in East Asia, Africa, and Europe. In the opening days of the war, Japan, one of the Allied powers, was tasked by Great Britain to take over German-held islands in the Pacific and land that Germany was leasing from China. At the end of August 1914, Japan seized the Mariana, Caroline, and Marshall archipelagos. On November 7, Germany surrendered to Japan the port of Qingdao and its Chinese leasehold. Neither Japanese victory entailed much actual fighting.

In Africa, the Allies (Britain and France, joined by Portuguese and Belgian imperial armies) fought to defeat Germany and take control of its colonies: Togoland and Kamerun (Cameroon) on the Atlantic's Gulf of Guinea, Southwest Africa (present day Namibia), and German East Africa (present day Tanzania, Rwanda, and Burundi). In addition, the Allies fought to end Germany's threat to Allied shipping in the Indian Ocean and the South Atlantic and to seize Germany's crucial war-support garrisons, coaling ports, and colonial shortwave stations. Germany's strategy in Africa was to put up such a good, determined, and lengthy fight to force the diversion of Allied troops from the western front to Africa.

The July 1914 completion of the construction of a strategic high-power wireless transmitter, a hundred kilometers inland from the Atlantic in Togoland, made that German colony the first to come under Allied gunfire. Its nine radio towers were a relay station for communications among Germany, its overseas colonies, the Imperial German Navy, and South America. The German army moved north to protect the transmitter as the British and French attacked southern Togoland. In the end, German technicians, ironically, destroyed the station to keep it out of the Allies' hands.

Kamerun was a more difficult struggle. The Allies were unfamiliar with the terrain; there were few roads; rivers lacked bridges; lack of transportation options necessitated prolonged marches; and military supplies seemed perpetually unavailable. The German side was short on men, munitions, and artillery. The eighteen-month campaign saw the Allies steadily pushing the Germans inland until they surrendered in February 1916. The battles in this campaign depended on more than 30,000 porters carrying what was needed for fighting: ammunition, guns, clothing, food, medical supplies, tents, and stretchers for the wounded. Working conditions were appalling: porters were not issued shoes or blankets; there was insufficient food; and although they were supposed to be paid, they often were not. They suffered the gamut of tropical diseases: malaria, yellow fever, sleeping sickness, blackwater fever, and guinea worms. An estimated 20 to 33.3 percent of West African porters died of job-related conditions.

In Namibia, the Allied struggle with the Germans lasted eight and a half months, ending in July 1915. Germany's chief antagonist was the Union of South Africa, part of the British Empire. South African forces crossed Namibia's southern border, the Orange River, and pushed the Germans north. The Germans reprised their erstwhile genocidal strategy of poisoning water holes; they also destroyed railroad tracks to complicate South African troop movements, making South African efforts heavily dependent on porters. In the end, it was another German defeat.

Primarily a guerrilla war with a few big battles but generally fitful fighting, the struggle for the Germans to retain control of their largest colony, German East Africa (GEA), technically continued for the full length of the war. The German Colonial Army, led by Major General Lettow-Vorbeck, was, throughout the war, small (his initial forces totaled only 2,750, including 2,500 African soldiers and 250 German officers, doctors, and noncommissioned officers). Lettow-Vorbeck's military genius lay in his being able to keep in check the 300,000 Allied troops with only up to 14,000 soldiers fighting for Germany (3,000 Europeans and 11,000 indigenous blacks). His GEA campaign was called "the greatest single guerrilla operation in history, and the most successful."[10] A brilliant guerrilla tactician, Lettow-Vorbeck adapted quickly to his environment, took advantage of German strengths, and exploited Allied mistakes. He raided British East Africa, northern Rhodesia, and Portuguese Mozambique, targeting forts, railways, and communication centers. Fluent in Swahili, Lettow-Vorbeck lost not a single battle in the four-year war and became affectionately known as the "Lion of Africa." Although he had served as adjutant to Trotha in the Herero war (though not in the genocide), he did not share his commander's racism. He appointed black officers and reportedly said, "Here in Africa, we are all equal. The better man will always outwit the inferior, and the color of his skin does not matter."[11] *I love this quote*

In this colony of 384,172 square miles, porters—men, women, and children—were more important and utilized than in other African colonial wars, and most were conscripted to do this work. Reportedly, in GEA, Germany used 191,700 porters; Britain, 1 million; Belgium, 260,000; and Portugal, 60,000, for a total of 1,511,700. The estimated number of porters who died on their treks is about 300,000; when one compares the number of dead porters with the numbers of soldiers who were killed in the warring armies—21,479—it is clear who was dying most in East Africa's killing fields. Roughly 93 percent of the dead were black African porters, not white European soldiers; yet, until recently, these porters have—shamefully—not been counted among the war's dead. As for the composition of European armies, the numbers of European whites were only a small percentage of the "European" armies. When Lettow-Vorbeck surrendered in late November 1918, his army was composed of 155 Europeans and 1,168 African blacks; that is, the German army was 12 percent European and 88 percent black Africans.

Not only did colonial lands become embroiled in the war but colonial subjects and other foreigners were brought or drafted into the European fighting as well. Up to 140,000 Vietnamese were drafted by the French to serve as laborers; roughly the same number was recruited from China; from India, as many as 600,000. On the western front, at least 50,000 Chinese and Indian laborers were killed. Some of them fought in battles with Ottoman forces and others with Allied troops seizing Germany's African colonies. Colonials were drafted to fight on the front lines in various theaters of war: 1.4 million Indians, 330,000 Australians, 640,000 Canadians, and 135,000 West Africans (from Algeria, Senegal, and Morocco). One million were drafted in the United States, though only about 500,000 made it to the front lines.

A maleficent harvest of war was the masses of refugees displaced both internally and across national borders—an estimated ten million in Europe. Statistics cannot convey the suffering and peril of flight and the often-bitter reception of refugees in areas to which they fled. One Belgian refugee put the reality bluntly: "We weren't real people anymore." The refugee tsunami overwhelmed localities and their plans and the financial resources to deal with it. Statistics can convey the enormity of the dislocation. Following the defeat of the Italians at Caporetto (November 1917) by the Central powers, 400,000 Italians fled from north to south. In the Hapsburg-Bulgarian invasion of Serbia in 1916, 500,000 Serbs followed the fleeing Serbian army across Kosovo and Albania to the Adriatic, a displacement that involved one-third of Serbia's prewar population. In the last German offensive on the western front in spring–summer 1918, 1.85 million Frenchmen fled into France's interior.[12]

The tried but untrue prediction at the start of any war is that "this [*little did they know* ☺] will be short." Offensive warfare throughout the nineteenth century had followed the strategy of pursuing the enemy to defeat him in a series of decisive battles. The critical forces in victory or defeat were the muscles of humans and horses. The problem by 1914 was that advanced military technology had made previous military tactics obsolete.[13] War was no longer a battle between forces fighting hand to hand with bayonets or with short-range guns. Rather it was a fight between two armies consisting of machines, specifically long-range weapons. Infantry rifles had a range up to one thousand meters (about five-eighths of a mile) and were deadly accurate at about five hundred meters (roughly three-tenths of a mile). Movable artillery used by armies in the field had a range of up to five miles and could now fire repeatedly without having to be re-aimed after each shot. Heavy artillery could hit targets over twenty-five miles distant and even farther; in 1918, Germans bombed Paris with long-range artillery from eighty miles away. Armies could thus be attacked well before they were aware of any enemy.

Military historians have shown that commanders on both sides spent much of the war's first three years trying to conquer with manpower (the old method) in what was history's first mechanized war. The new weaponry greatly increased the tempo and deadliness of combat, but communications technology was still primitive. Although machine guns, firing six hundred rounds per minute, did not come into use until after 1915, once they were available, they created an even more lethal situation. As for tanks, the British did not use them until September 1916, the French not until April 1917, and the Germans not until January 1918. It was not until the last year of the war that tactics and strategies more attune to the realities of mechanized warfare began to emerge. In this warfare, technology made the defensive far more powerful than the offensive, and that shaped the nature of war. Victories had to be rapid. If not, enemies could wind up in a stalemate—which is exactly what happened on the western front in France. The gap between technology and war strategy and tactics cost the lives of hundreds of thousands of men.

The reality of such firepower demanded protection for soldiers, and they dug a meandering trench system stretching seven hundred kilometers from the North Sea to the Swiss border. Between Allied and Central powers, trenches were no-man's lands ranging from seven yards to five hundred yards. The first German effort to break through the French, Belgian, and British forces at the Battle of the Marne in September 1914 failed, and the Germans were driven back to the line of trenches and what became the mostly stationary western front. Thus, from the beginning of the war, the hell of immovable armies was in place; six million soldiers served in these trenches throughout the war. Attempts to force the enemy back led to merciless slaughters in no-man's lands. Both sides made unsuccessful and immensely wasteful attempts to break through the other's line (the Germans at Verdun and the Allies at the Somme River—both in 1916—and the last-ditch German offensive in 1918). The ten-month Battle of Verdun took between 750,000 and 1 million lives; the four-month Battle of the Somme claimed the lives of about 1.1 million men.[14]

The medical system to deal with such horrific casualties had two battlefield levels. Near the frontlines were field dressing stations where the mortally and lightly wounded were brought; the lightly wounded were treated and returned to the fight. The seriously wounded were brought to casualty clearing stations (CCSs), far behind the battle lines, for diagnosis and emergency treatment, including amputation; by 1917, blood transfusions were routine. At the CCS, Marie Curie, who directed the Red Cross Radiology Service, set up on her own initiative two hundred X-ray units, which served about one million soldiers. In big battles, CCSs were swamped by huge numbers. Despite this system, many wounded were simply ignored or lost in the fog of war. A marked success in the

In July 1916, soldiers of the Second Indian Cavalry Division participated in the only cavalry action during the Battle of the Somme, successfully beating back the Germans. These skilled Inditman troops represent the global aspect of the war. Historical Images Archive/Alamy Stock Photo EC80X4

war were immunizations for infectious diseases: cholera, typhoid fever, and tetanus. Governments "drafted" large numbers of physicians from their own civilian practices: over 50 percent of all British doctors were mobilized and about 80 percent of German doctors.[15]

The Germans pioneered the use of deadly poison gas, but the Allies followed suit, and both sides used it freely. In 1915 it was chlorine gas, which could destroy the soldier's respiratory organs within seconds of inhaling. In 1916 came phosgene, which could kill through pulmonary edema or heart failure, often with delayed effect, and in 1917 mustard gas appeared: almost odorless, it was potentially lethal, causing serious external and internal blisters. The numbers of casualties from poison gas are impossible to calculate, but such deaths were ghastly. Poet-soldier Wilfred Owen, in "Dulce et Decorum Est," describes a soldier who suffered a poison gas attack and is thrown into a cart:

> He plunges at me, guttering, choking, drowning.
> If in some smothering dreams you too could pace
> Behind the wagon that we flung him in,

And watch the white eyes writhing in his face,
His hanging face, like a devil's sick of sin;
If you could hear, at every jolt, the blood
Come gargling from the froth-corrupted l
Obscene as cancer, bitter as the cud
Of vile, incurable sores on innocent tongues.[16]

Owen was born into a lower middle-class family in Shropshire in England's West Midlands. He passed the University of London entrance exam but did not qualify for a scholarship. Enlisting in a regiment of the British Army Reserve in 1915, he was commissioned second lieutenant in 1916. Field experiences in early 1917 led to psychic hospitalization for shell shock (today, post-traumatic stress syndrome). At the time, military authorities and even doctors saw the condition as a cover for cowardice or malingering; disciplinary action, public shaming, and even electric-shock therapy were prescribed for dealing with the symptoms. Owen was treated at a hospital where psychotherapy was used instead; he had shown an interest in poetry throughout his education, and part of his "treatment" was to express his wartime issues in poetry. He did so eloquently and has become one of the foremost antiwar poets in world literature. He was returned to the battlefield, where he was killed at age twenty-five, one week before the armistice ended the war on November 11, 1918. The closing lines of "Dulce et Decorum Est" offer his bitter verdict on war and patriotism/nationalism:

My friend, you would not tell with such high zest
To children ardent for some desperate glory,
The old Lie:Dulce et decorum est pro patria mori.[17]

(The Latin says, "It is sweet and seemly to die for one's country.")

While the western front stalemate continued, the British and Germans began to look for victory at sea. The mutual aim of England and Germany was an effective maritime blockade—England, with the world's strongest navy, and Germany, with submarines (U-boats). Germany had declared waters around the British Isles a war zone. However, when a German U-boat in May 1915 sank the passenger ship *Lusitania*, eleven miles off the southern Irish coast causing the death of 1,198 people, world reaction was enraged, especially in the United States. Therefore, Germany, not wanting to bring the United States into the war at that time, temporarily backed off from its hunt-and-sink policy. But in February 1917, it declared unrestricted submarine warfare, putting all ships at risk. That declaration and the sinking of several

American ships brought the United States into the war on April 6. With its ships and men, the US entry bolstered the Allies and played a substantial role in defeating the Central powers.

The United States entered the war three weeks after Tsar Nicholas II abdicated the Russian throne, the first step in taking Russia out of the war. Russia's wartime experiences were brutally bloody, militarily demeaning, and politically convulsive. In the first month of the war, the German army encircled and destroyed Russia's entire Second Army at Tannenberg, with 30,000 killed and 95,000 captured. In 1915, the Russians fled the invasion of German and Austro-Hungarian forces, in the Great Retreat: 2 million Russians were killed, wounded, or captured. In the perception of the middle class, businessmen, and intelligentsia, the principal problem lay in the mismanagement by and the corruption, conservatism, and waffling of the government.

When Nicholas II abdicated on March 15, a provisional government, mostly led by constitutionalists, took the reins of power. It was too little, too late. Events outran that regime's ability to deal with overwhelming problems. The St. Petersburg (Petrograd) Workers' Council (or Soviet), a mouthpiece of the most radical Social Democrats, the Bolsheviks, opposed the provisional government and demanded a quick end to the war. On November 6–7, 1917, the Bolsheviks, led by Vladimir Lenin, seized power and immediately opened peace talks with Germany. The Treaty of Brest-Litovsk (in modern-day Belarus) in March 1918 took Russia (and the Eastern Front) out of the war and acknowledged the independence of Finland, the Baltic states, Poland, and Ukraine.

The war's denouement ended the Ottoman, Austro-Hungarian, German, and Russian Empires. Great Britain, France, and Japan received former German colonies or spheres of influence. The postwar map revealed two new independent nations, Czechoslovakia and Yugoslavia, emerging from the collapse of the Austro-Hungarian and Ottoman Empires.

Yugoslavia, dominated by the Serbs, was the ultimate fruition of the goals of Princip's assassination of Franz Ferdinand. The Versailles Treaty of 1919 aimed to end the German threat, but it only ratcheted it up. The Allies treated Germany as an international pariah and criminal. Included in the treaty was a "war guilt" clause by which Germany "accepted the responsibility" *for all the destruction of the war*—the Allies demanded reparations for war damages, totaling US$846 billion in 2015 values. Germany reacted with bitter resentment. The Allies had sown the wind; they would reap the whirlwind, or, in a line by Wilfred Owen, "the foul tornado."

A major impact of the war was the transformation of the relationship between state and society. Total war brought the state unprecedented needs: manpower for the military and for labor; the assuredness that industrial production would not be hampered by strikes; preventing the hoarding of commodities; the control of imports, exports, and shipping in general; and censoring public statement to forestall undercutting the nation's wartime efforts. These issues demanded a greater degree of government planning, regulation, and intervention in the society and economy. Most states had not planned for resources because of the predictions of a short war that would have minimal impacts on daily life. Wartime economic difficulties—sharp spikes in inflation, high prices, and food scarcities—were often continual. Despite efforts to prevent labor unrest, strikes, including among troops, were prominent in 1918 in Germany, France, England, Italy, and Russia.

The tragedy of the war itself was punctuated catastrophically at its end by a pandemic of "Spanish flu" that infected 500 million people across the _dehumanizing the other side_ December 1920. The flu's spawning _– you don't know the enemy_ e, a large Allied staging-base-hospital co _you're killing_ soldiers, forty to fifty miles west of the scribed it as "a vast, dreadful encampme beasts are kept [a few days] before the Those infected at Etaples in the winter atory flu-like symptoms plus lavender-tin for this flu was 40 percent, eventually killing up to 100 million people around the world: it was history's deadliest medical catastrophe, far exceeding the fourteenth century's Black Death. Though influenza generally killed the elderly or the very young, a mutant strain in late 1918 to early 1919 generally cut down healthy young adults: in 1918–1919, 99 percent of influenza deaths were people under age sixty-five.

Sixty-three-year-old President Woodrow Wilson apparently caught the Spanish flu in early April 1919 when he was in negotiations at the postwar peace conference at Versailles. It may have altered his psyche in some ways. After the illness, the president's advisors noted his inability to grasp things quickly and that he was unable to remember in the evening what the council had done in the afternoon. It was also after the illness that Wilson gave up trying to dissuade French premier Clemenceau from laying the "war guilt" clause on Germany; before his illness, he had been determined not to let that happen. If such changes in psyche came from some neurological problems that the flu had set off, then the

Spanish flu, in claiming Wilson as a victim, perhaps changed the course of history beyond the disease and death itself.

Another older victim was the seventy-year-old former reformist president of Brazil, Rodriguez Alves. He had been reelected president with over 99 percent of the vote in November 1918, only to die two months later. He had worked assiduously for yellow fever and smallpox vaccinations in Rio, but, unfortunately for him and for all its victims, there was no influenza vaccine.

"What happens in Europe doesn't stay in Europe."

CHAPTER 2

Claustrophobia: Totalitarianism and the Great Depression, 1920–1936

Despite the temporarily devastating nightmare of the Spanish flu, a new day of hope arrived with the armistice. The interwar years glinted with prospects for peace—the war, after all, had been hailed as the one to end all wars, to make the world safe for democracy. There was faith that prosperity would return after the death and dearth of the war years; in the short run, this hope, at least in the rapidly modernizing regions of the world, seemed realized. But war's end was, tragically, a prelude to a quarter century of greater despair than hope. The hope for peace was inhibited in the following years by the flawed Treaty of Versailles and the establishment of the League of Nations, a weak global body unable to overcome the strong nations, which most leaders saw as the chief political units and actors at the time.

The modernizing world of the "roaring," the "golden," the "crazy" Twenties (adjectives dependent on particular cultures) was awash in consumerism: radios, telephones, movies, and especially the automobile. The millennium-old reliance on the horse was past, run over by the car and the revolutionary assembly line. In 1910 the Ford Motor Company could build a Model T in twelve hours; in 1914, it took one and a half hours. The total world production of automobiles in 1920 was 2.4 million, in 1929, 32 million. The Twenties were marked by technological breakthroughs: in aviation, Charles Lindbergh's transatlantic flight (1927) and British Royal Air Force Officer Sir Frank Whittle's patent for the jet engine in 1930; in communications, the 1923 invention of the television or cathode ray tube, the first transatlantic telephone call in 1927, the 1933 introduction of FM radio, the invention of radar

The Twentieth Century: A World History. Keith Schoppa, Oxford University Press. © Oxford University Press 2021.
DOI: 10.1093/oso/9780190497354.003.0003

in 1935; and in entertainment, the first "talking" motion picture (*The Jazz Singer*) in 1927 and the first color television transmission in 1928. World-changing medical advances during the Twenties included the discovery of insulin in 1921 and of penicillin, the world's first antibiotic, in 1928. Penicillin was called the "miracle drug"; before it was discovered, there was nothing to stop or heal infection—death might come from a minor wound, a blister, a scraped knee, or strep throat.

The war had shattered the status quo, opening up possibilities for new individual identities. From F. Scott Fitzgerald's *This Side of Paradise* (1920): "Here was a new generation . . . dedicated . . . to the . . . worship of success, grown up to find all Gods [sic] dead, all wars fought, all faiths in man shaken."[1] For many in their worship of success, the mania was money. It was a get-rich quick mentality, endorsed by Calvin Coolidge, who, as lieutenant governor of Massachusetts in a 1916 address to the Amherst Alumni Association, linked business with the power of religion and made the individual the worshipper: "The man who builds a factory builds a temple. The man who works there, worships there."[2] Cultural seismic waves from the Great War earthquake threatened traditional values; shaping the new world was thus a confusing challenge. For some it was a time for ending the repressive Victorian era; others clamored for mass consumer culture to homogenize different religious, ethnic, and cultural groups. Some called for expanding urban reforms, while many, fearful of social and political change, fought hard against moderate immigration policies and social pluralism.

Women were at the center of change, most active in their search for and selection of new identities. Many women focused initially on machines that made life easier: new electric appliances, washing machines, and vacuum cleaners. The hedonistic age of the flapper with its demand for personal freedom and license was perhaps best embodied by Josephine Baker, an African American singer and dancer. Growing up in the St. Louis slums, she lived on the streets, slept in cardboard boxes, rummaged through garbage cans for food, and barely supported herself doing street-corner dancing. At fifteen, she joined a black vaudeville group in New York. In 1925 she moved to France, where she took Europe by storm. Hemingway called her "the most sensational woman anyone ever saw. Or ever will."[3] She became the first world-famous black female entertainer and the first black woman to star in a movie. She would play more real-life political roles in World War II and after.

In the shaping of women's identity in the postwar world, change was global. In Japan *moga* (modern girls) strode the Ginza, Tokyo's central upscale shopping area, smoked, watched movies, and indulged in

Josephine Baker, an African American dancer from St. Louis, danced at the Folies Bergère in Paris in the 1920s and 1930s. A symbol of the freedom, even license, of young women in the Roaring Twenties, she was notorious for her scanty and suggestive costumes, including one made of bananas. Pictorial Press Ltd/Alamy Stock Photo C1FFY6 casual sex. Ding Ling, China's most important twentieth-century female author, wrote *Miss Sophie's Diary* (1927), a long short story, frankly exploring the title character's sexual uncertainties. In Berlin and other Western capitals, the most-chic hairstyle became the pageboy as the previous voluptuous feminine ideal of the woman was overcome by the garconne style, with more boyish figures and androgynous looks. In the political arena, Gandhi brought Indian women into the nonviolent civil disobedience movement. The Egyptian Feminist Union was founded in 1923; in 1925, primary education became compulsory for girls; and by the late 1920s, women went to universities.

The political plum women sought most directly and eagerly was the right to vote, but for many women in the world, that search was lengthy, ridiculed by men, and riddled by countless political obstacles and restrictions. Each country eventually achieved female suffrage, perhaps not with the assistance of support groups in their own or other countries but often at the same time as non-developed, poor states without clear political advantages. The timing, therefore, for success was unpredictable and sometimes surprising.

The earliest suffrage winners, from 1881 until 1919 were some polities from the British Empire and from Scandinavia—generally prosperous and politically progressive: the Isle of Man (1881), New Zealand (1893), Australia (1902), Finland (1906), Norway (1907–1913), Denmark (1915), and Sweden (1918). But there were also less developed countries from the Baltic region and Eastern Europe: Poland (1918); Estonia, Latvia, and Lithuania (1919, 1918, 1918); and Azerbaijan (1918).

The Nineteenth Amendment to the US Constitution gave US women the right to vote in August 1920. The United Kingdom also passed two laws in 1918 and 1928 to set female suffrage in place about the same time as the Americans. But in the 1920s, they were joined by notably lesser states like Mongolia (1924), Uruguay (1927), and Ecuador (1929). The 1930s followed suit: only one major state, Spain (1933), brought female suffrage into being; it was joined by Turkey (1930), Chile (1931), Thailand (1932), and Romania (1937). Surprisingly, some of the largest, most important world states did not recognize women's suffrage until the mid-to-late 1940s: France (1944), Italy (1945), Japan (1945), and India (1947). Most interesting was the late date in two Western European states for agreeing to female suffrage. Most of Switzerland settled on that decision in 1971, but one Swiss canton recognized women's right to vote only in 1991. Women in Portugal received this right only in 1976.

Beyond "flapperization" and the gradual opening of more opportunities for women, the work of American Margaret Sanger was path-breaking. Birth control activist, nurse, sex educator, and writer, she argued that women should be able to decide when to bear children. She opened the first American birth control clinic in 1916, founding the American Birth Control League in 1921. Constantly harangued by authorities, she was arrested for dispersing information on contraception, which broke US anti-obscenity laws.

She lectured frequently in American locales and in China, India, and Japan. But selling the idea of contraception was a perpetual uphill battle. In 1960 came the word that the female birth control contraceptive—"the pill"—was approved for use. But it was not until 1965, one year before her death, that the US Supreme Court decriminalized the use of contraceptives by married couples; unmarried couples did not gain that right until 1972.

Despite the wide range of new identities women could choose—housewife, mother, flapper, mass consumer, educated professional—older traditions and ideas persisted. A 1926 decree from Mussolini's government barred women from holding public office; Germany followed suit. Women's sole fascist social function became motherhood—Mussolini's dictum: "War is to man as motherhood is to woman." In 1927, Mussolini set a target of five children per family. The 1928 Amsterdam Olympic Games saw both a victory and a defeat for women. They were the first Games in which women could participate in track and field events. But after several women runners collapsed after the 800-meter run, women were banned from Olympic races longer than 200 meters until 1960. Traditional thinking still won the day; women continued to be seen as the weaker sex, an identity ascribed to them by most men.

Despite the cultural hoopla of the period with its attendant technological, medical, economic, and social achievements, the interwar years were remarkably claustrophobic with the erection of stifling, wall-like political, economic, and cultural structures and systems.

Nativism and xenophobia created parochial and paranoid attitudes that further shaped policies in many nations around the globe. In the United States, these were banner years for the Ku Klux Klan, of which 35,000 members paraded in hoods in Washington, DC, in August 1925. The United States, internationally isolated by an "America first" mentality and its refusal to become a League of Nations member, erected walls to keep out immigrants, first restricting the admission of "undesirables" from Southeast Europe in 1921, then excluding all Asians in 1924. In

Canada, campaigns to deport and disenfranchise black immigrants and to segregate public spaces rose spontaneously. In many European nations, including Sweden, France, Poland, and Austria, Jewish immigration from Eastern Europe was frowned upon. Japanese xenophobic reactions against outsiders in general came into focus after an immense earthquake struck Honshu, the largest Japanese island, on September 1, 1923. In the aftermath of the quake, which killed over 130,000 people, panicked Japanese accused "the other"—specifically Koreans and communists and radicals—of poisoning wells and vandalizing property. Vigilantes targeted Koreans, whose country Japan had colonized and whom the Japanese considered "low-life," murdering from 2,500 to 6,000. In tense times, the Koreans easily became the Japanese scapegoat. Communists and radicals vowed to change the "national essence"

The Ku Klux Klan parade in Washington, DC, in September 1926, with its fifty thousand marchers, demonstrated this national group's ongoing hostility to blacks, Catholics, and Jews. It was the second of two massive parades in consecutive summers; the one in August 1925 had thirty-five thousand marchers. Library of Congress Prints and Photographs Division, LC-DIG-npcc-16225 (*kokutai*); the government outlawed them in 1925, making participation in such groups punishable potentially by death. In every sense of the word, they were outsiders to the Japanese family.

Just as individuals, especially women, in the postwar world sought to establish new identities, so too did nation-states whose futures seemed threatened by economic chaos, disorder, danger, and crisis. A none-too-surprising backlash to the uneasy times was the development of two polarized totalitarian systems—communism and fascism—that offered models or identities that nations might select. Both systems gradually imprisoned their peoples within political and economic walls. The cataclysm of the Great Depression only bolstered the walls and deepened the danger of economic suffocation. Two men of literature, Lu Xun of China and Garcia Lorca of Spain, suggested ways of breaking down the ideological walls and ending the claustrophobia. Chinese commonly consider Lu Xun China's greatest twentieth-century author and social critic and is sometimes called the father of modern Chinese literature. He starkly posed China's social and cultural problems in 1922: "Imagine an iron house without windows, . . . with many people fast asleep inside who will soon die of suffocation . . . since they will die in their sleep, they will not feel the pain of death. Now if you cry aloud to wake a few of the lighter sleepers making those unfortunate few suffer the agony of irrevocable death, do you think you are doing them a good turn?" He continued, "But if a few awake, you can't say there is no hope of destroying the iron house." Hope of destroying the system (here, the Confucian system) lay in the individual's initiative (Lu Xun wrote to the second person, to "you") in striking out against or, at the least, standing up to the ideological, political, and cultural strictures that could lead to societal asphyxiation.

Lu wrote in the midst of Chinese military and political tragedy, in which warlords were plundering the Chinese countryside, producing untold death and destruction. The promise of a Chinese republic, established in 1912, had become a nightmare. In his "iron house" metaphor, Lu focused on the cultural and ideological straitjacket of patriarchal and paternalistic Confucianism, which many Chinese intellectuals blamed for China's humiliating weakness and which had to be demolished for any chance for Chinese progress. The solution to the iron house problem, according to Lu's story "A Madman's Diary," was the children, individuals not yet contaminated by the old culture. "A Madman's Diary" used the metaphor of cannibalism for how Chinese had demeaned, ostracized, and oppressed others in the name of Confucian values. The last lines of the story: "Perhaps there are still children who have not eaten men?

Save the children . . . "[4] Destroying the iron house and saving the children were calls to arms.

Russia's Bolshevik Revolution had stimulated the formation of communist parties in most countries of the world in the late 1910s and 1920s; from 1917 to 1923, several communist "revolutions" in Central and Eastern Europe failed. Fifteen Euro-Asian "republics" composed the Union of Soviet Socialist Republics (USSR), established in 1922, all controlled by the Communist Party headquartered in Moscow. Lenin was party and government leader from 1917 until his death in 1924. Though the party's ultimate goal was complete control of the economy, after years of terror and the turmoil of revolution, Lenin adopted the New Economic Policy (1921–1927), which allowed for a partial infusion of capitalism and which instigated an economic revival.

In the 1920s, Soviet Russia was in the vanguard of considering women's roles and increasing their social stature, exemplified by the establishment of the Zhenotdel (the Women's Department of the Communist Party) in 1919. A number of women led it during its eleven-year existence, but the most effective was Alexandra Artiukhina, a Bolshevik feminist, who served from 1925 to 1930. The department's primary goal was to help women adjust to situations in the new social order, specifically healthcare, daycare, and discrimination in the workplace. After growing up in a single-parent home, Artiukhina personally empathized with working-class women, for she had been a textile worker in St. Petersburg. Her charisma and speaking ability catapulted her to the board of the textile workers union at age twenty-one and to the city's Central Trade Union Bureau. She edited several journals, including *Rabotnitsa* (Working woman). Strong-willed and outspoken, she opposed the production of household electrical appliances, fearing that they would make women captive to housework. Save the money, she said, so that we "have the means . . . to throw into the construction of socialized institutions—cafeterias, nurseries, kindergartens, and laundries."[5] Under her leadership, Zhenotdel expanded all over the Soviet Union, where in Muslim Central Asian republics such as Uzbekistan the effort to assist women drew protest, outrage, and even the murder of women who participated. For all the good that it accomplished, Stalin abolished it in 1930—peremptorily announcing that the "woman issue" had been solved.

Stalin's First Five-Year Plan of 1928 revealed a much more radical scheme than the New Economic Policy. Although the goal of collectivization had been to increase agricultural output to pay for industrialization, it failed completely. Catastrophic mistakes and miscalculations undid the program of flipping the countryside's private landholdings into collective farms that essentially controlled every aspect of peasant life. Peasants violently resisted Stalin's revolutionary action by burning their crops, destroying machinery, and killing farm animals. Disruptive, "pie-in-the-sky" state policies and the destructive peasant reaction resulted in a deadly famine in Russia and Ukraine in 1932–1933. Stalin, in turn, deported those resisters to labor camps (Gulags: an acronym for Main Administration of Collective Labor Camps), mainly in Siberia, the Arctic north, and southern Central Asia. In 1930–1931, 1.8 million were sent to the Gulags, and some 400,000 died there. The Soviets began to send Poles there in 1932; 10 percent of the Baltic area population was deported there. From 1926 to 1939, in another mass population movement, because fewer workers were then needed on farms, about 20 million moved from farm to city. In Stalin's headlong run into the iron house of totalitarianism, conformity was the great virtue. In the mid-1930s, however, revolution began to cannibalize itself. Stalin held a series of show trials and bloody purges of his rivals or perceived rivals from 1933 to 1938. The state internal security apparatus later reported that between 1930 and 1953, 3.8 million people were sentenced for counterrevolutionary actions; more than 786,000 (21 percent) were executed.

Meanwhile in Europe, the political and psychological trauma from the Great War was strongest in Italy and Germany; both felt mistreated and alienated by decisions at the postwar peace conference in Versailles. Their reactions, in contrast to the USSR's turn to communism, tended to the far right in the form of fascism, a radical authoritarian nationalism, opposed to liberalism, Marxism, and anarchism. Many fascists believed that World War I, with its elevation of the power of the nation-state, had rendered liberal democracy obsolete and made totalitarian single-party states the answer to solving modern economic and military challenges. The rise of Italy's Benito Mussolini's beginning in 1922 combined parliamentary maneuvering with strong-arm tactics in a two-steps-forward, one-step-backward kind of approach. In January 1925, he dissolved Parliament and became dictator; his agreements and accommodation with the Church, especially in establishing a separate Vatican state, helped hasten—at least for Catholics—the acceptance of his growing totalitarianism. The rigidity of state control became more stultifying over time. Mussolini had his paramilitary ex-soldier Black Shirts bring any opposition into line through intimidation, humiliation, and sociopolitical pressures (use of censorship and propaganda, under radical political centralization). In 1931, all university professors and schoolteachers were required to swear a loyalty oath to fascism and to teach according to its principles. By 1934, all elementary teachers had to wear the black shirts of the Fascist Party in school. Though Italy's fascism was first to come to power, Mussolini's regime, in contrast to Germany's, was authoritarian but generally benign. Was this Fascism Lite?

With their emphasis on state power and national strength, Mussolini and the fascists set out to structure a new national identity, an Italian empire in northeast Africa, by invading Ethiopia in 1935. Though the League of Nations condemned the invasion as aggression, it took no strong action in response. Mussolini and others in the imperialistic Western world called it a "civilizing mission": Mussolini declared, "The war we began in the African land is a war of civilization and liberation." In May 1936, Italy annexed Ethiopia and joined it to Eritrea and Italian Somaliland to make Italian East Africa.

The Weimar Republic (1918–1933) was Germany's first experiment in democracy, but it proved to be a nightmare. Postwar hyperinflation reached the point in 1923 when it took one trillion marks to equal one US dollar. The serious economic crisis combined with postwar anger and bitterness produced a dangerous mix. On the one hand, it gave rise to a sense of political and cultural apathy (why bother saving when money was essentially worthless?) with a consequent surge toward general hedonism, a rapid rise in cocaine use, and a pronounced loosening of sexual morals. On the other hand, it led to denunciations of "moral decay," pointing fingers at the Republic as the main factor in both hyperinflation and social deterioration. The political upshot was that both the extreme right and extreme left gained strength in the late 1920s. By 1929, many Germans saw the Weimar Republic as illegitimate.

Then came the Wall Street crash of October 1929, which hit Germany harder than most nations, so dependent as it was on US finance. The subsequent Great Depression was the economy's decisive finishing blow and the springboard for the success of Hitler and Nazism. Marked by rancorous political turmoil, the months of January through March 1933 were critical for Hitler's rise to dictatorship. In that time, President Paul von Hindenburg named Hitler chancellor of the Reichstag; the emergency powers article of the constitution was invoked on the pretext that communists had allegedly set fire to the Reichstag; and the Reichstag passed the Enabling Act, which gave Hitler and his cabinet the authority to enact laws without legislative approval, including setting the budget and changing the constitution without the consent of the Reichstag. The Weimar Republic was dead. On July 14, 1933, the Nazi Party declared itself as Germany's only legal political party. In November 1933, Hermann Goring, whom Hitler had just appointed as minister president of Prussia, established the Secret State Police, the Gestapo.

From there, it was all an upward trajectory for Hitler (who had become a German citizen only in 1932) and his dictatorship—and straight downhill into the iron house of insanity for most of the Germans. On the Night of the Long Knives, in summer 1934, Hitler struck in twenty-one cities, sending execution squads to kill leaders of Nazi storm troopers (who had become difficult for him to control), some Nazi founders, and former government officials. Estimates of those murdered ranged from two hundred to more than one thousand. Then, on July 13, 1934, Hitler justified the purge in a nationally broadcast speech to the Reichstag: "If anyone reproaches me and asks why I did not resort to the regular courts of justice, then all I can say is this: In this hour I was responsible for the fate of the German people, and thereby I became the supreme judge of the German people."[6] One of the most ominous steps toward ultimate catastrophe was the Nuremberg Laws announced by Hitler in September 1935. Campaigns against Jews—boycotts and outright violence—had been an increasingly bitter undercurrent for several years, but now they were being codified into national policy. These laws forbade marriage and sexual intercourse between Jews and German Gentiles. In addition, all Jews lost their German citizenship, their national identity. In October 1938, Jewish passports were invalidated. Then came Kristallnacht, November 9, 1938, the Night of Broken Glass, when 7,500 Jewish businesses were trashed, 267 synagogues set afire, 91 Jews murdered, and at least 25,000 Jewish men jailed. Hitler called his regime the Third Reich (realm or kingdom), the First Reich being the Holy Roman Empire, and the Second Reich the empire created by Bismarck in 1871.

A fascist, militaristic Japan was not born out of Great War disillusionment; it had been a victorious Allied power in the war. Three major cultural and political realities and developments gave rise to a state in the 1930s that had many similarities to Germany and Italy. First was the centuries-long tradition of military rule in Japan: the era of the shogun and samurai, based on *bushidō* (the code of the warrior), lasted from the 1180s to 1868. Military values shaped Japanese identity, culture, and society. When that long era ended with the ousting of the shogun and the resumption of rule by the Japanese emperor in the 1868 Meiji Restoration, Japan threw itself headlong into modernization

In the aftermath of Kristallnacht, the Night of Broken Glass, in November 1938, two men pass a Jewish-owned store, the windows of which have been shattered by Germans during the night. The two men take in the scene without any evident surprise or anger. United States Holocaust Memorial Museum 86838

in the Western mode; in short, that meant industrialization, liberal reforms, and constitutionalism with a parliamentary government and competing political parties. Japan did all in its power to keep up with the Westerners in adding land to its empire, gaining Taiwan in 1895 as well as islands to the north of Japan in 1905. In addition, Japanese treaties noted after the war with Russia that Japan held "predominant rights" in Korea. That essentially meant that Japan could call all the shots in Korea. For example, Japan conducted a comprehensive land survey from 1910 to 1918 to establish property rights, but Japan made all the decisions, no matter how many Koreans lost their land. Because many farmers did not have documents that showed that they owned the land, many Koreans lost their source of livelihood. During World

War II, 40 to 60 percent of Korea's rice crop was sent to Japan, with Japanese making that decision without any feedback from Koreans. In a last example, the Japanese attempted to build a Shinto shrine in every village and force people to worship there. But Shinto existed in Japan, not Korea, where Buddhism held sway. This was then a failed effort to insert Japan's dominant religion into Korean religious culture.

The problem: Japan had moved much too quickly for many to be able to accept and adapt with equanimity to the sudden changes. In the new Japan, many people felt left out or left behind. Rural Japan was mired in poverty; it did not see any of the profits of modernization. Many intellectuals felt alienated: How did the new Japanese identity fit with its old military-based identity? What did it mean to be Japanese? Along with progress, then, came disgruntlement, jealousy, bitterness, and suspicion. The xenophobic and hysteric reactions following the Great Earthquake in 1923 pointed to the fragility of social and political equilibrium. In the 1920s, the new politics seemed to spawn corruption at a time when civilian political parties reduced military budgets. Even before the onset of the Great Depression, Japan struggled, starting as early as 1927 with serious bank failures. Suddenly, to many, especially in rural areas and military circles, the new Japan came to be seen as increasingly ugly. The old values associated with the military—loyalty, purity, courage—seemed to such groups the proper antidotes to the problems of the time.

After years of rule by regional military cliques and their leaders, known as warlords, Chinese military campaigns in 1926–1928, fueled by a fervent nationalism to unite China, seemed on the verge of victory. Japanese military leaders in Manchuria perceived Chinese nationalism as an ominous threat to their interests. In September 1931, they blew up train tracks on their own railroad line, blamed it on the Chinese, and used this "incident" to begin a full-fledged war against China. Their goal: to turn Manchuria, which they seized in 1932, into a Japanese puppet state, Manchukuo. Though the League of Nations condemned Japan as the aggressor, Japan thumbed its nose at the world and simply stalked out of the League. Over the next four years, Japan continued its military aggression on Chinese territory, first moving into eastern Inner Mongolia and then into northern China itself.

Domestic rule in early 1930s Japan has been called "government by assassination." The military was divided among those who believed that the ultimate road to military success was the Imperial Way, relying on traditional military values and reinvigorating the status of the emperor.

The other faction believed the key to military success was modernizing with the best up-to-date weaponry. This group held the most elite military offices, while the Imperial Way group felt aggrieved as the subordinate faction. This bitter rivalry resulted in the Imperial Way soldiers' attempting coups several times in the early 1930s; they failed, but their actions led to the assassinations of key civilian political leaders, bankers, and journalists. Then, in late February 1936, a mutiny led by the Imperial Way seriously threatened the government. The modernization faction, with the support of the emperor, put down the three-day mutiny. As Japan moved to total war with China in 1937, the "modern-weaponry" faction purged the Imperial Way and continued its march to military modernization.

In the midst of increasingly bitter political polarization in much of the world came the US stock market crash of 1929, when people around the globe, according to economist John Schumpeter, "felt that the ground under their feet was giving way."[7] Federico Garcia Lorca was in New York City at the time. He recalled, "I was lucky enough to see with my own eyes the recent stock market crash, where they lost several million dollars, a rabble of dead money that went sliding off into the sea."[8] The Great Depression followed. Most economists contended that the crash was not the cause, but rather the catalyst for the economic disaster that followed. They pointed to business troubles long before the crash: declines in production, the tightening of interest rates, and the rationing of credit. Installment buying had gotten out of hand. People purchased items on a plan that allowed repayment in small installments over time with added interest. If they lost their jobs, they could not repay the money and the purchased item would be repossessed. In the United States, where the depression was longer and deeper than anywhere else, the volume of installment paper outstanding (that is, the unpaid debt on installment loans) was $1.375 billion in 1925 and had more than doubled to $3 billion in 1929.

In the 1920s, the United States was mired in an agricultural crisis: during the Great War, American farms served as the breadbasket for Britain and France. This expanded production was not immediately cut back after the war, leading to a glutted market where prices that farmers received for their crops fell drastically; further, there was no way the already oversupplied market would buy the farmers' recently harvested crops. Between 1920 and 1932 one in every four farms was sold to meet financial obligations, and 600,000 farmers went bankrupt. For farmers in the United States, the Great Depression began when World War I ended.

The American urban boom of the 1920s had been built on the automobile, that is, the manufacture of vehicles (including tractors), tires and other components, gasoline stations, oil refineries, roads, garages, and suburbs. The production of automobiles plummeted from 440,000 in August 1929 to 92,500 in December 1929, a decline of 79 percent in four months.[9] By the end of the year, new car registrations fell almost 25 percent from September. Overstocked factories began to lay off workers. Unemployment skyrocketed to 25 percent, remaining over 17 percent in 1939, and not falling below 14 percent until 1941—whereas in most European countries, the unemployment rate fell back to normal (5 to 7 percent) by 1943. Consumers with less income created fewer demands for goods, which led to lower production and less demand for labor, leaving more consumers with less income and declining demand: it was a vicious cycle.

Two policy decisions made by governments to curb the cycle only made the situation worse. To protect those industries still producing and to improve the unemployment situation, countries began to raise tariff levels to keep out foreign-made goods. The result was that countries around the world retaliated by raising their own tariffs. International trade fell 40 percent, creating economic havoc in countries whose economies were based mostly on selling their raw materials or products. Countries in Latin America that provided pivotal raw materials or commodities were especially hard hit. In Chile, 80 percent of government revenue came from the exports of copper and nitrates. Now that these were in low demand because of the Depression, the lack of exports dropped the 1932 GDP to less than half of that in 1929. In Brazil, between 1929 and 1932, coffee prices fell from 22.5 to 8 cents a pound. Export prices collapsed in Argentina as well. The precipitous drop of US investments in South America worsened the situation. One result: social unrest, leading to the establishment of military dictatorships in Peru, Argentina, Brazil, Chile, and Uruguay.

Another policy decision that prolonged the Depression in some nations was the decision to stay on the gold standard, where the value of the currency was pegged to gold, for which it might be exchanged. Mainstream economists argued that since the money supply was thus determined by gold supply, at times of economic recession or depression banks could not expand credit fast enough to offset deflation. Countries that abandoned the gold standard in 1931, the United Kingdom, Japan, and the Scandinavian nations, recovered faster from the Depression. The so-called gold bloc of France, Belgium, the Netherlands, Italy, Poland, and Switzerland did not do so until 1935–1936 and took longer to recover.

Some countries were little affected by the Depression in the long term, among them Japan, China, the USSR, Spain, Portugal, and Greece, whose industry actually expanded during the period. Rebounding from the Depression began in most countries by 1933, but it was neither rapid nor widespread. Sweden was the first nation to fully recover. The Depression affected domestic politics in many countries. In the Balkans, it weakened forces of democracy, raising fears that parliamentary systems would not be able to handle the economic situation. In France, the Depression, while not especially severe, led to extreme political instability. Germany's economy was in considerable trouble. Its unemployment rate in 1932 was 30 percent; high unemployment was ended only when the economy was restructured for the huge program of military rearmament starting in 1935. Another part of Germany's money problems stemmed from its loan linkage to the United States. The Treaty of Versailles required Germany to pay war reparations, but it had no money. Banks in the United States joining with Allied economic institutions developed a plan in 1924 in which US banks issued bonds to private investors on behalf of Germany, which agreed to pay them off when the money came due. Charles Dawes, former director of the US Bureau of the Budget, chaired the oversight committee. In 1928, affected countries wanted to make the schedules for payments more permanent and established the plan headed by US banker Owen Young. Hitler canceled all reparations when he took power. Through the rest of the century, Germany acknowledged the reparations, and it paid off its last installment of interest in October 2010.

British dominion nations suffered economically, with consequent political unrest. The bottom dropped out of the wool market in Australia and New Zealand, leading to 20 to 30 percent unemployment. Canada's industrial production dropped 58 percent from 1929 to 1932. In England itself, the northern industrial base was economically stressed with unemployment in some areas even reaching 70 percent; the Midlands and southern England were much less affected.

In the hard-hit United States, the Dust Bowl exacerbated the severity of the Depression. By the mid-1930s, some 350 million tons of topsoil had been blown from the Great Plains to the East Coast. This natural disaster stemmed ultimately from a change in weather patterns with the Pacific becoming colder and the Atlantic growing warmer; the jet stream running from west to east across the United States dipped farther to the south where it produced precipitation, rather than as usual on the Great Plains. The situation resulted largely from no or very little rain, much heat and wind, and longtime farming practices. Once

This dust storm on April 18, 1935, hit the town of Stratford in the northernmost part of the Texas Panhandle. Traveling across the region, the storms caused serious ecological and agricultural damage. The most severe turned the day dark, and people called them "black blizzards." NOAA, George E. Marsh Album

farmers had settled in the Great Plains, they wanted more land for cultivation: they plowed nearly 5.2 million acres of prairie grasses that had protected the topsoil. The ground was thus bare, and the high winds easily picked up the rich topsoil and blew it east.

For the presidency of Franklin Roosevelt (1933–1945), the Depression created political turmoil between traditional conservative capitalist supporters and those who believed that capitalism could be saved only if the government took action as the ultimate protector of the public well-being. Though FDR's New Deal programs were pragmatic attempts to deal effectively with the catastrophic economic situation, in the end, as in Germany, the Depression was effectively ended only by the huge military expenditures of World War II.

In the historical landscape of the 1930s, no nation in Europe touched so many raw nerves as Spain, in which the left (workers, unions, and peasants) and the right (landowners, the Church, industrialists) struggled for power. The policies of the Second Republic, born in 1931 after a decade of dictatorship, were shaped first by liberal/left ideology: liberals generally believed that the central problem of politics was protecting and enhancing the freedom of the individual and that government was necessary to protect individuals, especially the disadvantaged, needy, those discriminated against, from being harmed by others or by various forces in society. In reaction to two years of liberal rule, the forces of the right (conservatives) were elected in 1933; they usually were connected to the economic and social elites and stood for limited government, free markets, personal responsibility, and individual liberty. Then in reaction to conservative rule, the more determined left won the elections in February 1936, a result that led directly to civil war. Touched off by a revolt of right-wing Spanish military officers in Spanish Morocco in July 1936, it spread quickly to mainland Spain.

It was during this period of social and political turbulence (1932–1936), that Garcia Lorca wrote three of his most caustically cruel plays depicting the evils of Spanish culture: *Blood Wedding* (1932), *Yerma* (1934), and *The House of Bernarda Alba* (1936). He was an avant-garde member of the "Generation of '27," writers who brought cultural ideals prevalent in European literary circles—surrealism, futurism, and symbolism—into Spanish literature. But these three plays focused not on European literary ideals but on specifics of Spanish culture that seemed to Garcia Lorca brutal, cruel, and frighteningly claustrophobic. A socialist, he was fervently opposed to the right's agenda and to dictatorship, and these plays touched on his emotions and ideology. All three dramas focused on family and generational issues and on gender and sexual relations. The central conflict is between conservative and uncompromising Catholic morality (that served as the determining factor in each play) and instinctive human feelings, desires, and passions. Garcia Lorca believed that conservative and Catholic forces damn people to lifelong unhappiness and depression. All the plays end in tragedy—specifically in bloody killings. Against these forces of ideological oppression, Garcia Lorca, like Lu Xun, spoke of individual action as the spark that could break down the iron walls or tear apart the "souls of leather."

For Garcia Lorca, the key was *duende*, a word he used particularly to relate to the arts of dance (specifically flamenco), music, and poetry. In a 1933 lecture he gave in Buenos Aires, Garcia Lorca explained: "I heard an old maestro of the guitar say: 'The *duende* is not in the throat: the *duende* surges up, inside, from the soles of the feet! Meaning, it's not a question of skill, but of a style that's truly alive: meaning, it's in the veins; meaning, it's of the most ancient culture of immediate creation.' "[10] In a broader sense, *duende* can be defined as a quality of passion and inspiration. The seemingly intractable, suffocating political, social, and cultural walls could be handled, Lu and Garcia Lorca seemed to say, by the actions of individuals passionately inspired to demolish them. Against communist and fascist prisons or the strangling death grip of the Great Depression, such duende might seem powerless. But both Lu and Garcia Lorca suggested that there is no other choice.

Several months before his death, Garcia Lorca mused specifically about his perspective on himself as an individual based in his locality with his own prescribed kin and social linkages, his relationship to his nation, and his relationship to the global community—a central theme of this book.

> I am totally Spanish, and it would be impossible for me to live outside my geographical boundaries. At the same time I hate anyone who is Spanish just because he was born a Spaniard. I am a brother to all men, and I detest the person who sacrifices himself for an abstract, nationalist ideal just because he loves his country with a blindfold over his eyes. A good Chinaman [sic] is closer to me than a bad Spaniard. I express Spain in my work and feel her in the very marrow of my bones; but first and foremost, I'm cosmopolitan and a brother to all.[11]

For Garcia Lorca, the end came too soon. On August 19, 1936, at age thirty-eight and at the height of his own artistic *duende*, he was kidnapped by Nationalist militia a month after the start of the Spanish Civil War and executed. It is not clear whether he was murdered for his belief in socialism or because he was homosexual or for both. Neither his bones nor his grave have been found to this day. Two months to the day of Garcia Lorca's death, Lu Xun succumbed to lung cancer in Shanghai. Silent were the voices of these men who had championed the role of the individual in relation to the nation-state, its breadth of power, its ability to exact taxes, its capacity to place various commitments and obligations on its citizens, and its often-muddled socioeconomic strategies.

CHAPTER 3

Worlds Blown Apart, 1937–1949

The Spanish Civil War, in its polarized ideology, unrestrained violence, ethnic animosity, and terrors of modern military technology, was a harbinger of World War II. The war was an ideological struggle between the left and right. In a Europe already increasingly similarly polarized, fascist Germany and Italy sent infantry, air force, and armored units to support the nationalists, led by General Francisco Franco. The USSR backed the Republicans, mainly through advisors. The fascists' more tangible and accessible aid helped bring victory to Franco, who assumed power in March 1939 and held it until 1975.[1]

The carpet bombing of Guernica, a town of seven thousand in the Basque country of northern Spain, on April 26, 1937, was the first such raid by a modern air force on a European civilian population. Guernica was utterly destroyed. Such aerial destruction in world history had first been a tactic used by colonial powers in their colonies or would-be colonies: Italy in Libya in 1911–1912, Britain in India's northwest province in the late 1920s and 1930s, and Italy in Ethiopia in 1935–1936. In any case, it showed a terrifying face of twentieth-century warfare waged in both backyards and battlefields.

Commissioned by the Republican government to do a painting for the Spanish pavilion at the 1937 Paris World's Fair, Pablo Picasso created the gray, black, and white painting *Guernica*, showing, in effect through its Cubist style, a world being blown apart. On the seventy-fifth anniversary of the painting, journalist Alejandro Escalona stated, "*Guernica* is to painting what Beethoven's Ninth Symphony is to music: a cultural icon that speaks to mankind not only against war but also of hope and peace."[2] The dozen years, 1937 to 1949, saw many worlds blown apart in addition to Guernica: the prewar order in Asia and in Europe, the long-time control of Palestine by the Arabs, the collapse of the British

The Twentieth Century: A World History. Keith Schoppa, Oxford University Press. © Oxford University Press 2021.
DOI: 10.1093/oso/9780190497354.003.0004

At the beginning of the Spanish Civil War in 1937, Spanish dictator Francisco Franco had the support of fellow fascist states, Germany and Italy, which began a bombing campaign to extend Franco's power. They chose the town of Guernica as the April 26 target because it was the base of Basque culture, which Franco distrusted. They destroyed 70 percent of the town, killing and wounding 1,600 civilians (a third of the population). World History Archive/Alamy Stock Photo EX6XAW

Raj (the Hindi word for "rule") in India, and the prewar global political and economic institutional framework.

In 1919, the Soviet Union established the Communist International (Comintern) to direct communist movements around the globe. Most successful in China, it initially supported both the Nationalist Party of Sun Yat-sen and the Communist Party (eventually led by Mao Zedong). In the mid-1920s, the two parties worked together in a united front against warlords and imperialists. After Sun's death from cancer in 1925, the Nationalist Party drifted into the hands of right-wing politicians, as a military campaign to unite the country was being waged. Jiang Jieshi, commander of that campaign, seized power and purged the communists, ending the united front in 1927–1928. The communists regrouped in peripheral areas of the southeast, forming the Chinese Soviet Republic in 1931. Jiang launched four "extermination" campaigns against the communists before the success of the fifth in 1934. As a result of the communist loss, about 100,000 people fled on the Long March, a roughly six-thousand-mile trek to Yan'an in far northwest China, where they sought to rebuild and expand their power.

When the terrifyingly brutal invasion of the Japanese began in July 1937, the two sides joined once more in a united front against their common enemy; but that lasted only until 1941 before rivalry and bitter enmity between the two destroyed the united front. In both north and central China, Japan's initial campaigns were marked by terror, biological and chemical warfare, and the massive bombing of cities. Japan's scorn and hatred of the Chinese undergirded such brutal military tactics. The judgment of Japan's Major General Sakai Ryu, chief of staff of Japanese forces in north China, went from bad to worse: "China is a society, but she is not a nation. Or rather, it would be fair to say that China is a society of bandits. The Chinese people are bacteria infesting world civilization."[3] The most notorious was the so-called Rape of Nanjing, the Chinese capital, which saw mass murder of civilians and countless rapes in late 1937 and early 1938. In response to communist resistance in the north in 1940, the Japanese launched a vicious "kill-all, burn-all, loot-all" vendetta, where all Chinese were fair game for unrestrained terror. All in all, an estimated twenty million Chinese died in the war.

In Europe, Hitler's drive to total power through war seemed unstoppable. *Time* magazine named him Man of the Year in 1938 as he moved to make ready "killing fields" in Europe and the USSR. As Germany expanded in its rise to world power, Hitler's ultimate goal was to establish an Aryan empire from Germany to the Ural Mountains. Aryans were a mythical prehistoric people who were said to have spoken an archaic Indo-European language.[4] By the early twentieth century, the customary understanding of the original Aryan people was that they were powerful, white-skinned conquerors, who moved aggressively south into Persia and India and west into Europe, defeating and humiliating the "substandard" races they confronted and establishing a powerful empire. Nazis taught that these early Aryans basically established civilization and culture. However, they continued to be energetic and on target with their lives only so long as they maintained the "purity" of their race. If, for example, they married slaves or any one of the "lesser" races, they became, as it were, contaminated and sank to a contemptible and shamefully weak racial level. That outcome had apparently materialized for the Aryans of India, Persia, and the Slavic nations, and, to a lesser degree, those of Southern Europe. Supporters of Aryanism came to view the Nordic and Germanic peoples as the purest members of the "race."

Hitler wanted to expand the living space available for Germans and the whole Aryan "race." He considered the land from Germany to the Urals the natural territory of the German people, an area to which they were rightfully entitled. The huge size of this tract of land is suggested by the 2,246 miles between Berlin and Yekaterinburg in the eastern Urals. This land would be the "living space" (Lebensraum) that Germany needed so badly for Hitler's pan-Germanic empire. That empire was expected to assimilate almost all of Germanic Europe into a hugely expanded Reich. Territorially speaking, this included the existing German Reich itself (consisting of pre-1938 Germany proper, Austria, Bohemia, Moravia, Alsace-Lorraine, and German-occupied Poland), the Netherlands, the Flemish part of Belgium, and at least the German-speaking parts of Switzerland and Liechtenstein.[5]

A key component of the Nazi "Plan for the East" were the Jews who inhabited what was formerly called the Pale of Settlement, an area in western Russia designated in the 1790s by Catherine the Great as the homeland where all Jews in Russia should live. In 1900, the Pale had the largest concentration of Jews in the world, about five million, representing 40 percent of the global Jewish population. The Pale lay in the present states of Ukraine, Belarus, Moldova, Lithuania, and parts of Latvia and Russia. In addition, neighboring Poland had the second-largest Jewish population in the world: 20 percent of all Jews lived there (90 percent of whom were killed during the Holocaust). The Jews along with the Slavic populations of southeastern Europe—peoples that the Germans, as the "master" Aryan race, had determined were inferior genetically, physically, and mentally—were to be killed, enslaved, or deported. Their lands, emptied of the "undesirables," were to be repopulated by Germans.

Hitler's wartime strategy was to deal with his Western enemies before those in the east to be able to focus ultimately longer on the east as he extended the Third Reich and opened up the settling of Lebensraum. In 1938, he annexed German-speaking Austria and the Sudetenland, seizing all of Czechoslovakia in March 1939. Then he embarked on full-scale war, achieving victories each year like clockwork: in 1939, the conquest of Poland; in 1940, the "lightning war" (blitzkrieg) across Northern Europe, capturing Denmark, Norway, Belgium, the Netherlands, and France. In blitzkrieg, Hitler deliberately avoided infantry-heavy assaults that had caused the World War I quagmire, favoring instead the speed and devastating power of his tanks, the heart of the German attack. But tanks could not cross the English Channel.

The Battle of Britain, beginning in the summer of 1940, was the first major campaign fought entirely by air forces; Germany's strategy was to use the bombing campaign to compel Britain to negotiate a peace settlement. Instead, it became Hitler's first loss. Although the bombing initially targeted airfields and infrastructure, the Germans eventually turned to terror bombing of civilians, causing about forty thousand deaths and more than fifty thousand casualties. Yet because it achieved and maintained air superiority, the RAF (Royal Air Force) continually bested the German Luftwaffe as Britain held firm in the air campaign.

Germany's invasion into the Soviet Union in 1941 thrust that country onto the Allied side. Hitler saw the invasion as crucial for his plan to depopulate the western Soviet Union to make more living space for Germans. He told his generals that this campaign was "a war of extermination" and that it was to be fought with no rules at all—except to kill as many people as possible.[6] That was Hitler to his troops. To his enemies, he was all lies, secrets, deception, malevolence, and betrayal. In December 1939, Hitler wired a message to Stalin on his sixtieth birthday: "Best wishes for your personal well-being as well as for the prosperous future of the peoples of the friendly Soviet Union."[7] In September 1941, a directive to his officers, written in the third person, put his true face forward: "The Fuhrer has decided to erase the city of Petersburg from the face of the earth. I have no interest in the further existence of this huge population center."[8]

Estimates suggest that by the end of 1941, some two million Russians were dead. With a wartime total of twenty million dead, the USSR suffered more than any of the Allies. As many Russians died during the siege of Leningrad (1941–1944) as all the soldiers and civilians killed in the United States, Britain, and France combined. In its major contributions to the war effort, the USSR remained suspicious of its Western allies, embittered that it had to stand up almost alone against Germany from 1941 until D-Day, June 6, 1944. Stalin had pushed for the invasion of Normandy already in 1941. He viewed the delay of action in France, which came principally from Churchill and the British, as a betrayal and a deliberate undermining of the Soviet Union. When they finally occurred, the landings at Normandy were the beginning of the war's end in Europe. Attitudes toward Jews were negative not only in Germany but all over Europe. At a conference on refugees in Evian, France, in July 1938, not a single European country was willing to take in Jews fleeing persecution. The United States agreed to take only a few over 27,000. In mid-October Germany expelled 12,000 Polish Jews living in Germany. Poland accepted only 4,000, with the remainder forced to live out on the German-Polish frontier. In June 1939, the *St.*

Louis, a ship with 907 German Jews, sailed to Havana, the passengers planning to make Cuba their home, but a sudden change in visa laws prevented almost all from disembarking. The United States refused to give the ship permission to dock in Florida. Forced to return to Europe, the ship carried at least a quarter of its passengers to their deaths in extermination camps. Jewish leader Chaim Weizmann rued the fact in 1936 that for all Jewish people the world "is divided into places where they cannot live and places into which they cannot enter."[9]

Just sixty-seven days after he was named chancellor in 1933, Hitler and the Nazi government promulgated a law that ordered those in government positions who had at least one Jewish grandparent or a Jewish spouse or were political opponents of the Nazi Party to be immediately dismissed. Tens of thousands of people—teachers, police officers, judges, and academics at top universities—were suddenly unemployed. In the next few years, thousands of German scientists and intellectuals fled to

When Soviet soldiers arrived at Auschwitz, there were at least seven hundred children and youth prisoners, including about five hundred under fifteen. More than half of these were Jewish. A forensic medical commission found that the majority were underweight and suffering from diseases acquired in the camp: 60 percent showed vitamin deficiency and overall weakening of the body, and 40 percent had tuberculosis. INTERFOTO/Alamy Stock Photo FFYKX9

the United Kingdom, the United States, and other countries mostly in Western Europe to protect their lives and livelihood. This forced brain drain meant that the Nazis and Germany were pushing out their own leading researchers, scientists, and intellectuals—not a minor loss, to be sure. But it was a major gain for countries to which they fled.

Thirty well-known physicists, Albert Einstein among them, fled to the United States; thirty-six, including Edward Teller and Erwin Schrodinger, went to England. Many physicists who came to the United States became major contributors to the Manhattan Project, the US government project (1942–1945) that produced the atomic bomb: Enrico Fermi, Max Born, Leo Szilard, Hans Bethe, and Einstein. All together by 1944, more than 133,000 German Jewish emigres had come to the United States, many of them well educated in the sciences. Of fourteen particularly well-known physicists, three had already received the Nobel Prize before leaving Germany and five more would win it subsequently. Physicists today claim that it is no exaggeration to say that the emigres from Nazi Germany "revolutionized U.S. science and technology."[10]

After Hitler annexed Austria in 1938, Lise Meitner, a brilliant Austrian physicist, felt compelled to flee to Sweden. Although born into a Jewish family, she had converted to Protestantism—in reality, a meaningless "conversion" viewed through Hitler's obsession with ineradicable Jewish identity. In Germany, Meitner worked with chemist Otto Hahn exploring radioactive substances; indeed, she was the scientific leader of the project that ran from 1934 to 1938. The first year of the project, they had to work in a remodeled carpenter's shop because the university did not yet accept women on an official basis. After she left Berlin in the summer of 1938, she encouraged Hahn to carry out the major experiment without her. They were the first scientists to recognize that when the uranium atom is bombarded by neutrons, the atom splits, and most often the fission process produces barium and krypton. They thus discovered the radiochemical proof of nuclear fission.[11] From Sweden she frequently consulted Hahn, offering her opinions and advice through her physicist's perspective; they met once in Copenhagen for a longer period to work together.

Perhaps, in an unfortunate reprise of Marie Curie's bouts with gender bias, Hahn won the Nobel Prize in Chemistry in 1944 but he did not even acknowledge Meitner's leadership and work on the project. Although Meitner had been accepted into the Hahn family through friendship and Meitner was godmother to Hahn's daughter, Hahn apparently was incredibly fearful of indicating that he had collaborated with a Jew. He wrote her letters about his reaction; he chalked it up to political fears: unspoken were Hahn's own personal ambitions and his gender bias. Meitner's contributions were at least acknowledged to a degree when she received a very high forty-eight nominations for a Nobel Prize between 1937 and 1948, when she and Hahn received the US Fermi Prize in 1966, and posthumously in 1997, when chemical element 109 was named Meitnerium in her honor.

Although the flights from Germany by academics were not what they had planned, the process of having to assimilate and work with others in a different cultural context played a role in extending globalization—both for the Germans and for their new host cultures. One of the German émigrés' largest commitments was to Turkey. The Turkish Republic had been established in 1923 by Mustafa Kemal Ataturk, who served as president until his death in 1938. Ataturk was determined to modernize and secularize the former caliphate. In the late 1920s, he instituted reforms, installing female suffrage and setting up a free and mandatory primary education system. Istanbul University had been an on-again off-again institution since 1453; in the early twentieth century, it had been mostly moribund. Ataturk had a great interest in seeing higher education flourish as a way to hasten modernization. The 1933 German law that forced German officials and academics with blood ties to Jews to stop working was a good thing for Ataturk and Istanbul University. Ataturk invited many German professors, especially science scholars, to come to the university and other educational institutions to give Turkish academics support, to offer classes, and to be models for research efforts. Almost two hundred professors arrived in a short period of time, with forty-two going to Istanbul University by the end of 1933. By war's end, about three hundred German professors went to teach, work, and serve as consultants in Turkish institutions.

For all Hitler's brutal military conquests, wartime genocide became a curse not only for World War II but also for the entire twentieth century. Even during the war, it was not limited to the Jewish Holocaust. In April–May 1940, Soviet forces mowed down an estimated 22,000 to 25,700 Polish military and police officers and intellectuals, burying them in mass graves in the Katyn Forest in western Russia. The murders, carried out under direct orders of the Soviet Politburo that were signed by Stalin, were politically inspired, but among the dead were some 900 Jewish victims.

Devastatingly horrifying was Germany's "final solution" to the Jewish "problem." Heinrich Himmler, a chief architect of the Holocaust, elaborated: "Antisemitism is exactly the same as delousing. Getting rid of lice is not a question of ideology. It is a matter of cleanliness."[12]

Viewing the Jews as scapegoats for Germany's humiliation in World War I, Hitler pondered: "Should I not also have the right to eliminate millions of an inferior race that multiplies like vermin?" The Nazis had many different "camps," among them prison, hard labor, concentration, and extermination—the latter, designed simply to kill people immediately. There were eleven extermination camps, seven in Poland, and one each in Ukraine, Belarus, Croatia, and Serbia. By one count, the number of exterminated Jews, Slavs, gypsies, homosexuals, Jehovah's Witnesses, communists, political dissidents, Soviet prisoners of war, and the "disabled" totaled 3,427,008, but the total as compiled from available sources is above 11,000,000.[13]

Altogether, about six million Jews were killed, almost half in towns and villages of the former Pale of Settlement (recently called "Bloodlands" by one historian),[14] Poland, Hungary, Romania, Yugoslavia, and the USSR. Cities and towns were burned, women were raped, and the Germans killed Jews in hideously inhuman ways, often murdering them on the day they seized the town. When the Germans conquered those in the Pale in June 1941, there were reportedly 2,700,000 Jews living there; twenty months later in February 1943, only 250,000 remained—a shockingly low 9 percent survival rate. The massacres at Odessa, Nikolaev, and in Transnistria in 1941 were carried out by Romanian occupation forces; those in Kaunas, the capital of Lithuania, by Lithuanians; the Germans later killed 70,000 more Jews in Kaunas, many from Western Europe.

In the Pale, Kovel—a western Ukrainian city during the war, today in eastern Poland—experienced the deaths of about twenty-seven thousand Jews. In the summer of 1942, Nazi forces locked about one thousand Jews, who had tried to escape, in the Great Synagogue to await their murders. In fear, anger, and terror, the prisoners scratched messages on the synagogue walls with pencils, pieces of porcelain, and shards of glass and stones. One, Tania Arbeiter, wrote for her "and all her family" on August 23, 1942: "Hush, the murderers are coming. Silence reigns in the hall . . . . Hearing their voices stops our hearts beating. Lord, take us to Your eternity! But the murderers will surely still pay with their blood! How will I be able to rejoice if I am already in the grave? But I wished that their every last child would be cut up into pieces while still alive. . . . Farewell my beautiful world, the world I did not have time to get to know."[15]

Auschwitz survivor Elie Wiesel, winner of the 1986 Nobel Peace Prize, perhaps best described the sorrow and depression: "Never shall I forget that night, the first night in camp, which has turned my life into

Residents of Leningrad painstakingly secure water from a broken pipe in December 1941. The winter of 1941–1942 was brutally frigid, snowy, and icy in Leningrad, which the Germans besieged for almost a year and a half. Obtaining food and water in these conditions was not always possible, but was, in every case, an exhausting process. Photo by V. S. Tarasevich. Russian State Film and Photo Archive one long night. . . . Never shall I forget the little . . . children, whose bodies I saw turned into wreaths of smoke beneath a silent blue sky. Never shall I forget those flames which consumed my faith forever . . . . Never."[16]

In their large conquered territories, Japanese and Germans had to rely on local collaborators to assert and assist in their rule. Those who chose to collaborate did so for many reasons: some believed that by collaboration enemy treatment of localities and their population would be less harsh and aggressive; others sensed that they could gain economic, social, and political advantages.

Others, like Yuan Zhulin, collaborated because they had no choice. Yuan, a Chinese woman born of poor parents in the central city of Wuhan, was a collaborator of sorts. In spring 1940, with her husband far away in the Chinese army, she was offered a job to clean at a provincial hotel. Jobs were difficult to find at the time, and Yuan agreed, only to find she had been assigned to a comfort station—a brothel—for Japanese soldiers. She was given a Japanese name and a room of about eight square meters, holding only a bed and a spittoon. The first day, ten Japanese soldiers raped her. "We girls who suffered numerous rapes every day needed to wash our bodies, but there was only a wooden bucket for us to take turns using. There were dozens of comfort women at the station, so the bath water was unbearably dirty by the end of each day."[17] Although the Japanese soldiers were ordered to use condoms, they did not. Yuan became pregnant, had a miscarriage, and then became barren for the rest of her life. Ramifications of her sex slavery would come to have even more ravaging effects in the 1950s (discussed in the next chapter).

Certainly more infamous were high-powered political collaborators. Vidkun Quisling was the Nazi collaborator serving as prime minister of German-occupied Norway; he cooperated with Hitler's genocidal policies as practiced in the final solution. He was executed by firing squad in October 1945. Probably the most infamous Nazi collaborator was France's Philippe Petain. It was, at minimum, ironic that France's greatest World War I hero became an enemy collaborator. After the German invasion, Petain became premier of France in 1940, signed an armistice with the Germans, and established a collaborationist seat of government from 1940 to 1944 at Vichy, 224 miles southeast of Paris. He willingly and actively participated in deporting French and non-French Jews to Nazi concentration camps, many to Auschwitz and Birkenau. For his willing collaboration with the Nazis, he was tried for treason by the High Court in Paris and condemned to death in August

1945, a sentence commuted to life imprisonment on the Ile d'Yeu (off the west coast of France) owing to his advanced age and his World War I contributions.

In contrast to Petain, Josephine Baker, the African American singer-dancer who immigrated to France in 1925, chose to support the Free French resistance led by General Charles de Gaulle. As an entertainer, Baker could easily move about Europe, carrying messages to the Allies with information on German troop levels in western France and on important airfields and harbors. Since the Free French had no organized entertainment arrangements for their troops, Baker and her friends did so on their own, allowing no civilians in the audience and charging no admission for their shows. After the war, she received the Croix de Guerre and the Rosette de la Resistance from De Gaulle.

The war in the Pacific began with the Japanese surprise attack on the US Navy installation at Pearl Harbor, Hawaii, on December 7, 1941. From the Japanese perspective, this was a huge expansion of the war they had been fighting in China since 1937. It also brought the United States into the war on the side of the Allies. Although Japan had some initial successes in the South Pacific, the turning point in the war came just six months after Pearl Harbor at the Midway atoll in the mid-Pacific. The United States won a smashing victory, sinking four Japanese aircraft carriers and other ships as well. The war in the Pacific dragged on after the European war ended on May 8 (following Mussolini's execution on April 28 and Hitler's suicide on April 30).

When US forces took Saipan in the Mariana Islands in the summer of 1944, its planes could reach Japan. They rained horrendous fire-bomb destruction on sixty-seven Japanese cities, built of wood that exploded in flames as quickly as kindling. On one night, March 9, 1945, US bombers burned to death 100,000 civilians in Tokyo with napalm bombs (made of jellied gasoline). The temperatures in the city ranged between 600 and 1800 degrees Fahrenheit; the heat was so intense that it melted asphalt, so torrid that people who went to canals to cool off were instead boiled alive. The firebombing destroyed 51 percent of Tokyo, the size of New York City; incinerated 58 percent of Yokohama, the size of Cleveland; and obliterated 40 percent of Nagoya, the size of Los Angeles.[18]

Then, in a shocking lack of proportionality following the vengeful and genocidal firebombings, came two atomic bombs: on August 6, Hiroshima; on August 9, Nagasaki. The number of people killed outright totaled up to 220,000. That number was made more tragically horrific by the thousands who later suffered radiation and gamma ray

The charred remains of Japanese civilians littered the streets after the United States conducted Operation Meetinghouse, the single most destructive bombing raid in all of human history, on the night of March 9–10, 1945. American bombs destroyed sixteen square miles (ten thousand acres) of central Tokyo, leaving an estimated 100,000 civilians dead and more than a million homeless. Photo by Ishikawa Kōyō via Wikimedia Commons

poisoning and died painfully. But the entrance of the Soviet Union into the war on Japan on August 8 had much greater impact on the Japanese than did the atomic bombs. Since the late eighteenth century, when Russian ships were the first to sail in northern Japanese waters, Japan had had an inordinate fear of Russian aggression. The specter of the Soviet army plunging unimpeded down the Korean Peninsula with the possibility of imminent invasion was chilling to Japanese policymakers.

After receiving news of the Nagasaki bombing, the six-member Supreme Council for the Direction of the War came together to discuss surrendering. They split their vote three-three on whether to agree to "unconditional surrender." The dropping of a second bomb changed no minds. The emperor (who had no vote) expressed his view that Japan should surrender. Given the overwhelming cultural, mythical, and religious power held by the emperor, his was a suggestion that could not be refused. Therefore, the "war party" could save face in effect by hiding behind the emperor's wishes. From 1945 until 1952, the United States occupied Japan and led it on a surprisingly liberal political path.

At the end of the world war, two British colonies in its dying empire, Palestine and India, were about to be changed forever. The nation of Israel was born at the turn of the twentieth century. In 1897, Austrian writer Theodor Herzl formed the World Zionist Organization to establish "for the Jewish people a legally assured home in Palestine." At the time, a few thousand Jewish farmers had immigrated and had generally been assimilated. In 1899, Yusuf Diya Pasha al-Khalidi, former mayor of Jerusalem, wrote to Zadok Khan, the chief rabbi in France, who was a friend of Herzl: "Good Lord, ... there are still uninhabited countries where one could settle millions of poor Jews who may ... one day constitute a nation. That would [be] the most rational solution to the Jewish question. But in the name of God, let Palestine be left in peace."[19]

In the early twentieth century, Arab opposition to Zionism grew increasingly bitter. Arabs argued that Jews who had previously lived in Islamic lands and assimilated into those cultures had always been accepted. Zionists, they argued, were Europeans obsessed with an imperialist mentality that justified conquering and dominating non-Western peoples and their territories. Unfortunately, however, by World War I the outlines of a tragic conflict that would extend well into the twenty-first century had already been drawn. In November 1917, the British Foreign Secretary Lord Arthur Balfour issued his "Declaration": "His Majesty's Government view with favor the establishment in Palestine of a national home for the Jewish people ... , it being clearly understood that nothing shall be done which may prejudice the civil and religious rights of existing non-Jewish communities in Palestine." As written it was simply a statement of British support for a certain policy, but it took on "legal" status when the League of Nations adopted it in the British Mandate for Palestine in 1922.

For Arabs, the very concept of a "mandate," which noted that these "peoples [were] not yet able to stand by themselves under the strenuous conditions of the modern world," was insultingly condescending.[20] The Arabs had stood by themselves for more than a millennium. A major unknown in the Balfour plan was the extent of Jewish immigration to Palestine. For the Jews, immigration was key for achieving majority status and completing the Zionist dream of a Jewish state. For Arabs, the ultimate tragedy was losing majority status in a territory they had dominated since the seventh century. The persecution of Jews during the war years coupled with the anti-Jewish closed doors of other countries compelled the British to allow more Jews to immigrate to Palestine. Whereas Jews comprised 11.1 percent of the population in 1922, by 1947 they made up 32 percent. From the Arab perspective, Jews were being persecuted by Christians in Europe, not by Arabs, but the Arabs were being made to pay the price.

In 1936, Arabs launched a revolt against the British to seek their own independence. Part of the uprising was an increasingly violent peasant resistance movement that targeted the British, who responded brutally. At least 10 percent of Palestinian males between the ages of twenty and sixty were killed, wounded, imprisoned, or exiled. The insurrection ultimately affected the outcome of the 1948 Palestine war, because from this point the British began to aid Zionist paramilitary units, especially the Haganah, which became the central force in Israel's national army.

In early 1947, Britain turned the Palestinian issue over to the United Nations. The UN formed a special eleven-member committee on Palestine, seven of whom voted for the partition of Palestine into two states—Arab and Jewish—and the internationalization of Jerusalem. A three-member minority report, supported by Muslims, advocated an undivided Palestine with limited local government for Jews. In November 1947, the UN General Assembly voted in favor of partition: thirty-three for, thirteen against, and ten abstentions; 72 percent of the voting members in the Assembly favored partition. But the UN Security Council refused to enforce the General Assembly plan, arguing that both sides must agree before going ahead. In the face of this decision, Britain withdrew from Palestine as fighting erupted between Arabs and Jews.

The day before the final British withdrawal on May 15, 1948, Jewish leaders declared Israel an independent state. On that day, five Arab states (Palestine's four neighbors, Egypt, Transjordan, Syria, Lebanon, and noncontiguous Iraq) sent military forces into Palestine. The war that followed continued into the first half of 1949 and was an on-again, off-again affair that ended with separate bilateral armistice agreements with the four neighbors, without settling any political issues. Whereas the 1947 partition had left Jewish Palestine with 56 percent of the territory, the 1948 war left Israel with 78 percent of the former British Mandate. The implications of the 1948 war were huge for both the Palestinian Arabs and Israel. What had been a clash between Arab and Jewish communities in the British Mandate now became an intrastate struggle. While Israel gained international recognition (apart from Muslim and Arab states) and UN membership, the Palestinian state envisioned in the 1947 partition plan was never established. The armistice lines from the 1949 agreements became, in effect, the accepted international borders until the Six-Day War of 1967.

Perhaps the most tragic result of the war was the beginning of an enormous Palestinian refugee problem. The British estimated that from 1947 to 1949 the number of Palestinian refugees totaled between 600,000 and 750,000. A Palestinian journalist offered this judgment: "The nation of Palestine ceased to be. Its original inhabitants ... were dubbed Arab refugees, sent regular food rations by the UN, and forgotten by the world. . . . [It was] the tragedy of another people who suffered for no reason, ... uprooted from their homeland."[21]

India, part of the British Empire in South Asia since the eighteenth century, posed as great a quandary as Palestine; part of the situation arose from Britain's arrogance and blundering. Assuming its "natural" colonial control, Britain drafted 1.4 million Indians to fight on the Western Front in World War I and another 600,000 to serve in labor battalions—altogether 2 million Indians served in Europe. In April 1919, at Amritsar in the Punjab region, about 10,000 men, women, and children came to the walled Jallianwala Gardens to celebrate a Hindu festival. Because of recent local incidents of dissent and retaliation, a British general had banned any public gathering. Once the festival was underway, the general suddenly ordered his troops to shut the exit gates and to fire without warning on thousands of trapped people. Four hundred Indians were killed outright; 1,200 more were wounded. The British governor of the Punjab celebrated the "incident," and the general, though relieved of his command, returned home to England as a hero who "saved" the Punjab for Britain. It was the logic of arrogant imperialism and of the callous disregard for the lives of the colonized; to this day, the British have not apologized for this despicable action of a century ago, much to the chagrin of Indians in that region.

Such incidents only heightened the Indian desire for independence, any thought of which gave rise ominously to fears of an inevitable struggle between Hindus and Muslims in a post-Raj India. Both groups were part of the Indian National Congress, a political party formed in 1885 with the goals of having Great Britain give Indians more representation in the government and of having Britain and India negotiate to steadily empower India as a colony. The Muslim League was formed in 1906 with British encouragement to "divide and rule" the Indian people as Hindus and Muslims. The British urged Muslims to start separate organizations; the League was specifically meant to be a foil to the Congress. The British imperialists, far from wanting a united India, maneuvered to sow the seeds of separatism and communal hatred.

Two lawyers in the Congress Party, trained in Great Britain, emerged as spokesmen for communal interests: Mohammed Ali Jinnah and Mohandas [Mahatma] Gandhi. In the 1890s, Gandhi served as legal counsel for a leading Indian entrepreneur in South Africa, where Gandhi first saw blatant racial bigotry. The situation stimulated Gandhi's consciousness of his Indian identity, giving rise to his idea of satyagraha, "holding fast to the truth," through nonviolent civil disobedience and noncooperation. He became head of the Congress Party in 1921, expanding the party beyond elites to include the poor, women, and the lowest caste, the untouchables. Whereas Gandhi spoke of the unity of Hindu and Muslim as "the breath of our life,"[22] Jinnah left the party (after a dispute with Gandhi) to focus on invigorating the Muslim League.

In the early 1920s, the British viceroy attempted to appeal to middle-class Indians by abolishing tariffs on cotton. In order to make up that lost revenue, he doubled the salt tax, thereby setting up a deeply regressive tax for the poor. In 1930, Gandhi focused on the salt tax as a test case for his satyagraha. With seventy-eight representatives from every region and religion in India, he set out to walk from his commune in western India 240 miles to Dandi on the Arabian Sea. After reaching the sea, he picked up a lump of salt and encouraged Indians everywhere to break the British tax law. The British responded with mass arrests: Gandhi was imprisoned, an action that only increased his stature among Indians. Not all of the Congress party supported Gandhi's view of the future: an India based on self-sufficient local communities and traditional values. Gandhi's acknowledged political heir, Jawaharlal Nehru, brought different priorities; he thought science and technology, not traditional structures and values, were the keys to India's economic and social modernization.

British policy vacillated between brutal repression of Indian resistance and gradually allowing Indians more political rights, a contradictory policy that led to uncertainty and instability. The 1935 Government of India Act established independent legislative assemblies in provinces and princely states, a national bicameral parliament, and the protection of Muslim minorities. However, when the British attempted to force India into World War II to do Britain's bidding, Indians reacted strongly. Under Gandhi's leadership, in August 1942 the "Quit India" movement demanded immediate withdrawal of the British and threatened nationwide civil disobedience. The British again crushed the movement, jailing

Gandhi and Congress Party leaders even as troops from India again came to Britain's assistance in the European war.

The end of the world war brought the end of the British Raj. After a turbulent 1946 when communal violence exploded between Hindus and Muslims, the British government, financially exhausted, decided in early 1947 to end its rule in India. The partition of India into two countries, India and Pakistan, led to the establishment of the Dominion of Pakistan with Muhammed Ali Jinnah as governor general and the Union of India with Jawaharlal Nehru as prime minister. This was the tragic drama concocted by the British: continuing to play their communal game, they pitted each side continually against the other.

The most destructive tragedy was already unfolding: sectarian violence tore the country apart in a horrifically bloody civil war. The partition of India and Pakistan led to 500,000 deaths, though estimates range from 200,000 to 1 million. Muslims in India who moved to Pakistan and Hindus and Sikhs in Pakistan who moved to India totaled 14.5 million—the largest mass migration in human history.

On January 30, 1948, Gandhi was assassinated by a militant Hindu nationalist upset with Gandhi's concern for Muslims. Nehru mourned: "The light has gone out of our lives and there is darkness

Fleeing India for Pakistan in September 1947, Muslims climbed onto the tops of train cars to look for any open spot. Many times mobs targeted and killed passengers traveling in either direction. AP Photo 470919023

everywhere."[23] India and Pakistan were now set on separate paths, freed from the British and both closely associated with their religion. They were still on the same subcontinent with Pakistan straddling India on two sides; there would be more troubles ahead.

Amid the worlds blown apart in the Spanish Civil War and World War II, the formation of the state of Israel, and the communal strife in India and Pakistan, visions of a new international world order were taking shape. Apart from the ineffective League of Nations, which was to have brought nations together to prevent another world war, the prewar world had seen nations competing with nations, nations mutually raising higher and higher tariffs, and nations turning inward to protect their own national industries. As a result, world trade plummeted disastrously. To deal with these problems that had fueled the Great Depression, in 1933 sixty-six nations met at the World Economic Conference in London. But the conference collapsed when Roosevelt opposed currency stabilization, so that each nation was left to recover on its own, as nationalism, not global innovations, carried the day.

Another conference, at Bretton Woods in New Hampshire in July 1944, was the follow-up to the failed London meeting a decade earlier. It aimed to overcome some interwar problems by constructing international solutions so that nationalism, always tricky to control, might not run amok. Guided by the aim of open markets, 730 delegates from forty-four nations met to establish systems to regulate the postwar international monetary and financial order. Its chief accomplishments were as follows: the formation of the International Bank for Reconstruction and Development (IBRD), the establishment of the General Agreement on Tariffs and Trade (GATT) to regulate international trade, and the founding of the International Monetary Fund (IMF) to promote stability of exchange rates and financial flows. These organizations or their successors remained active into the twenty-first century. The World Trade Organization (WTO) replaced GATT in 1995. The IBRD was the original World Bank, providing loans to developing countries for capital programs.

The Dumbarton Oaks Conference (August–October 1944) formulated proposals for the United Nations. Delegates from the US, the UK, the Republic of China, and the USSR met at the historic estate in Washington, DC. Founding negotiations for the United Nations began in San Francisco in April 1945, and twenty-nine members ratified the charter that October. The charter established the International Court of Justice (the World Court) at The Hague, Netherlands, to settle legal disputes between states and to offer advisory opinions on legal questions involving international agencies and the UN General Assembly. Bretton Woods and Dumbarton Oaks represent the first successful, concrete institutional steps toward globalization, which continued to develop through the century.

CHAPTER 4

A New Day? Revolution, Cold War, and Decolonization, 1950–1965

At lunchtime on February 28, 1953, at the Eagle Pub in Cambridge, England, Francis Crick, a British molecular biologist, interrupted the pub's patrons' lunch to announce that he and American James Watson, also a molecular biologist, had "discovered the secret of life." No, Crick was not drunk, and it was no idle boast; they had analyzed the double helix structure of deoxyribonucleic acid (DNA), the main constituent of chromosomes. Scientists the world over widely recognized that this was one of the most important scientific discoveries, not only of the twentieth century but of all time. It is noted, as well, that this was a groundbreaking event for biology, genetics, and our understanding of life itself. It thus became possible to discern how genetic instructions can be held within organisms and passed on to succeeding generations. The discovery ushered in six decades of biological revolution. Today the pub serves a special ale to commemorate the discovery, dubbed "Eagle's DNA."

In the early and mid-1950s, polio was a frightening global public health problem because it had no identified causes or cures. The peak of the epidemic in the United States was 1952, when 58,000 cases were reported, of whom 3,145 died and 21,269 were paralyzed. Then in 1955, Dr. Jonas Salk, a researcher at the National Foundation for Infantile Paralysis, discovered and developed the first polio vaccine. Before the vaccine, there were an estimated 600,000 cases around the globe every year; in the century's first half, it neared pandemic proportions in Europe, North America, Australia, and New Zealand. Once approved in an elaborate field test involving more than 2 million people, Salk vaccine was rushed around the globe with great urgency and swift results. In 1961, Dr. Albert Sabin begin to commercially produce an oral

The Twentieth Century: A World History. Keith Schoppa, Oxford University Press. © Oxford University Press 2021.
DOI: 10.1093/oso/9780190497354.003.0005

vaccine, which became even more desired than the Salk injection vaccine, especially in the developing world due to ease of administration. On the whole, the Salk vaccine was deemed safer: his vaccine was made up of dead polio virus, while Sabin's was alive, although a weakened polio virus. Sabin's vaccine remained potent a shorter amount of time than Salk's, and Sabin's sometimes produced intestinal problems.

Poliomyelitis has been historically endemic in China, with periodic epidemics documented since the early 1950s. Control of this devastating disease was an early public health priority for the newly formed People's Republic of China (PRC) on October 1, 1949. Standing on Beijing's Gate of Heavenly Peace, Mao Zedong proclaimed: "We, the 450 million Chinese, have stood up and our future is infinitely bright." "Infinitely bright"? This was in the face of the huge task of reconstructing the nation, a war in Korea, and the roughly 20,000 Chinese who died or were permanently paralyzed every year from polio,

First came the victory over polio. In 1953, strict surveillance of clinical polio cases was set in place; localities reported to the national level every year as part of a notifiable diseases reporting system. The new government clearly wanted to be seen in charge of what was happening in the nation's localities. The immediate need was vaccines to keep polio in check; the Salk vaccine came out in 1955, but the PRC could not get any because the United States had a technology blockade against China.

The Chinese government and the World Health Organization (WHO) have credited Gu Fangzhou, an important medical scientist and virologist, with eradicating polio in China. The Sabin polio vaccine was a liquid to be swallowed; to Gu and others, the oral vaccine made more sense than injections in dealing with vast numbers of people. But there were two problems in using the liquid vaccine: in vials it had to be stored at 2 to 8 degrees Celsius for the vaccine to maintain optimal potency. In the 1950s, however, many areas of China did not have electricity at all or had it in fits and starts—nor was there any equipment to maintain the low temperatures needed for the vaccine. Gu's goal was to vaccinate children, but the Sabin liquid vaccine did not taste good—and children often refused to drink it. In 1962, Gu developed the vaccine in the form of a more palatable sugary pill that children were eager to take. Once the pill was available, cases of polio in China dropped precipitously. The WHO praised Gu and China for pioneering the basic anti-polio strategy for the Western Pacific region: the surveillance program, strengthening the routine immunization system, providing supplemental oral vaccines in targeted areas, and stipulating national immunization days.

The day when Mao declared "we, the 450 million Chinese, have stood up . . . " was the culmination of three years of bloody civil war between the communists led by Mao and nationalist forces of Chiang Kai-shek that was fought at the same time as the revolution was unfolding in northern China. The nationalists had been beaten and demoralized, and nations around the world were recognizing Mao's regime as the legitimate government of China. And the victory had come without any substantial assistance from the Soviet Union. The West, however, far from seeing these developments as Mao did, saw the communist victory simply as proof of communism's unbounded aggression.

One of Mao's sobriquets, the "Red Sun," underscored that metaphorically a new day had dawned, seemingly presaging good fortune after a century of poverty, weakness, and humiliation. The new day certainly came in the successful struggle against polio, but setting the nation on the right path to reconstruction and building institutions for China's new state was harder to realize. In fact, during the first decade of the PRC, the country edged unknowingly toward calamity. Mao believed that the road to industrialization was through bumper agricultural harvests, which would provide the money to fund industrial projects (thus trying to duplicate Stalin's late-1920s plan). It necessitated larger and larger collective farms, where widespread mechanization would decrease the need for physical labor and might help increase output.

In 1958, Mao launched the Great Leap Forward, an attempt to equal the industrial output of Great Britain within fifteen years. A central part of the Great Leap was establishing communes, each made up of about 5,500 households, which served as the chief governmental unit in localities. Private garden plots and livestock ownership were forbidden; salaries were paid on a per capita basis, not on the basis of labor contributions. A crucial aspect of the Great Leap was setting up at least one million "backyard" iron smelters. Mao, the populist, believed that if the people became "hands-on" in industrial production, China could modernize more quickly because the people would have a direct stake in such progress. Some negative results of this unrealistic program were having farmers run the round-the-clock smelter schedule, which took them away from farm duties, and the large-scale deforestation for wood to keep the smelters sufficiently hot. The worst outcome was that the high-carbon pig iron produced from the metal items contributed by the people—iron tools and implements, window and bed frames, pots and pans—cracked easily because of faulty manufacturing techniques. Useful daily items had been rendered useless: on this basic level, the Great Leap toppled flat on its face.

The same year the Great Leap began, the World War II comfort woman Yuan Zhulin (discussed in the previous chapter), living in her native city of Wuhan, found herself in trouble. Her life as a comfort woman ended with the war, but one day her mother, with whom she lived, was at a neighborhood meeting called "Tell Your Sufferings in the Old Society and the Happiness in the New." Yuan's mother naively talked about Yuan's horrible experiences when she was forced to be a comfort woman. With the word out in public, people began to taunt Zhulin, screaming, "A whore working for the Japanese!" When the all-important Neighborhood Committee received the news, they accused her of having been a prostitute working for the Japanese (as if she had confessed this of her own accord), confiscated her house, and condemned her to hard labor for seventeen years in exile in Heilongjiang Province, about 1,500 miles to the northeast. The comfort station tragedy thus did not stop for Yuan at war's end.

The utter failure of the PRC's ironmaking experiment and its ripple effects on the economy were compounded by a deepening agricultural calamity. In cases of political one-upmanship, communes competed with other communes to produce the most abundant harvest, inflating the projected harvest by unbelievable amounts, and, as a result, they were showered with public praise. The central problem: when the state assessed taxes, collected in the form of grain, the amount of tax was based on estimates of the harvest. Since the estimates were so high compared to how much was really produced, the state ended up taking most of the grain, with only a little left for the many suffering from malnutrition and starvation.

Suffering from malnutrition, a person's body began to swell with the collection of fluid under the skin that turned yellow. One popular remedy was eating chlorella, supposedly a source of rich protein. Chlorella fed on human urine, so people stopped going to the toilet and peed in spittoons instead; then they dropped the seeds in. They grow into something that looks like green fish roe. In several days, the chlorella was scooped out of the urine, washed, and cooked with rice. It tasted truly disgusting, but it reduced the body's swelling.

Malnutrition could quickly degenerate to starvation. Overall Chinese mortality rates, which had averaged 11.1 per 1,000 in 1957, climbed to 14.6 per 1,000 in 1959 and shot up to 25.4 per 1,000 in 1960. The best estimates are that 30 million people died of hunger in this worst famine in human history (known as the Great Famine)—brought on by government policies that bordered on sheer lunacy. Even worse, the government did little to respond to the crisis, providing almost no assistance. The depth of the tragedy is revealed by the fact that per-capita food production would not reach its pre-1957 level until the early 1970s. It was the first PRC dark age—but an even darker one was on the horizon.

The US detonations of the bombs at Hiroshima and Nagasaki inaugurated the nuclear age. It continued with frequent tests of weapons as new nations joined the "nuclear club" before 1965: the USSR (1949), the United Kingdom (1952), France (1960), and China (1964). Both nuclear tests and the space race were hallmarks of the Cold War competition between the United States and the USSR. The Soviet Union launched the space age in autumn 1957, placing the first two satellites (sputniks) into orbit. With men circling the globe and walking in space, competition in these years (the 1950s into the early 1970s) followed a general pattern of Soviets first, Americans second. However, after initially leading the United States in space, the USSR failed in efforts to land men on the moon, while the US Apollo project succeeded with six manned moon landings from 1969 to 1972. The nuclear and space races reflected national rivalries, sharply different ideologies, and a growing distrust over issues of policy.

In the late 1940s, the Western goal was to "contain" the Soviet Union; with this aim in view, twelve nations established the North Atlantic Treaty Organization (NATO) in 1948. The USSR countered NATO with the Warsaw Pact (1955), composed of the Soviet Union and seven of its Central and Eastern European satellite states. The Allies had divided Germany into four zones of occupation, each headed by one of the Allies. Berlin was situated in the Soviet-occupied zone; in line with the country's division, the city was divided into four Allied zones. The rather sudden Soviet blockade of Berlin in 1948 seemed to the West a "black-and-white" issue of outright Soviet aggression.

Yet, from Stalin's perspective, he had watched German developments in 1947 and early 1948 as the three zones (headed by the United States, Britain, and France) had amalgamated into one economic unit with more political authority given to pro-Western elite Germans. Stalin believed that the West was edging toward politically integrating the three zones into a West German state, dependent on and loyal to the United States. If this integrated zone came into being, it would contain 75 percent of the German population and what had been the most productive industrial region in prewar Europe. Since Truman had reinstituted the draft in the United States and pushed strongly for NATO, it was clearly possible that a West German state could become a launching pad for US

Astronaut Buzz Aldrin peers at the Moon's Sea of Tranquility, where the lunar-module-lander, called the Eagle, had set down. This first moon landing occurred on July 20, 1969. To the right of Aldrin's feet are several instruments for initial research on the moon. NASA

aggression against the USSR. Hence, the Soviet blockade of Berlin and the clear Allied response, the Berlin Airlift.[1]

The Soviets blockaded all land and canal access to the western section of Berlin where two million people were, as a result, deprived of food, water, heating fuel, medicine, and other supplies from June 1948 to May 1949, when the Soviets lifted the blockade. Planes took off from England, in the beginning supplying five thousand tons of goods per day; near the end the tonnage reached eight thousand per day. The airlift carried 2.3 million tons of cargo in all, valued at $224 million.[2]

Cargo airplanes landed at Berlin's Tempelhof airport every four minutes. The Berlin blockade and airlift has been called the first battle of the Cold War.

The enmity and distrust between the Soviets and the Americans produced a cataclysmic episode in October 1962, the Cuban Missile Crisis, that brought the world an instant away from nuclear disaster. In 1959, Fidel Castro, an anticommunist before the United States rejected his advances, had seized power from ultra-rightist Cuban dictator Fulgencio Batista, whom the United States had fervently supported from 1952 to 1959. Castro moved steadily to closer relations with the Soviet Union. In April 1961, a CIA-directed invasion by the United States to take down Castro failed miserably. In the fall of 1962, Soviet leader Nikita Khrushchev, correctly suspecting another US invasion attempt, announced the dispatch of Soviet troops and technicians to Cuba to build missile sites from which to target the United States. Photographs taken from an American U-2 plane revealed launch pads for nuclear ballistic missiles. Between October 15 and 28, a tense confrontation brought the world perilously close to nuclear war. President John F. Kennedy imposed a quarantine of Cuba to prevent any further de-livery of arms and supplies, stating that any nuclear missiles launched from Cuba would bring a "full retaliatory response upon the Soviet Union." In the end, Khrushchev backed down, his authority weakened, and he was ousted from power in 1964. But the episode underscored the fragility and dangers of nuclear weapons that had the capacity to destroy global civilization.

Ironically, at the same time that long-term Western political empires were crumbling, the Cold War created for the United States and the Soviet Union new empires of nation-states based on ideological, polit-ical, and economic ties (social scientists today call these "client states"). These countries were economically, politically, and militarily dependent on another more powerful country (in this context, the United States and the USSR). Both empires attempted to attract and maneuver de-veloping states from Africa and Central and South America into their orbits. For the USSR, these included the Warsaw Pact nations, as well as Angola, Mozambique, Afghanistan, Cuba, and North Vietnam. The US long-term client states included Guatemala, El Salvador, South Korea, South Vietnam, Saudi Arabia, and the Philippines. With the end of the Cold War in 1991, relationships between the states in these ephemeral Cold War "empires" changed markedly.

The collapse of empires and the consequent appearance on the world stage of new African and Asian nation-states, in a process called decolonization, became a global trend in the 1950s and 1960s. Japan had built an empire quickly in the first two decades of the century, subsuming Korea, taking over Manchuria and ruling it as a puppet state (Manchukuo), and seizing the former German islands in the Pacific and German rights in China's Shandong province. Japan lost its empire with its loss in the world war, but the aftermath of that loss led to more war in its former colony of Korea. Although Japanese rule in Korea was harsh and brutal, after World War II Korea was free in its independence and nationhood. But what seemed like a new day turned more complicated because the northern part of the peninsula evolved into a state supported primarily by the Soviet Union and the southern part was a state dependent on the United States. This Cold War set-up meant that any military action by the North would be judged in the West as confirmation that communist aggression was on the march. The main issue and motivation for both the northern and southern regimes were their strong desire for the establishment of one independent nation on the peninsula, not that communism was pitted against capitalism and the Western way.

North Korea invaded the South in June 1950. In the three-year hot war (1950–1953) that followed, the frontline moved up and down the peninsula. Fighting North Koreans was a UN force composed of soldiers and medical support from twenty-two nations.[3] What made Westerners certain of their hypothesis of a worldwide communist conspiracy was the support the North received from the USSR and the PRC. China's commitment was remarkable, for its undertaking was massive and exceptionally costly. Coming as it did only eight months after the end of the civil war and the establishment of the PRC, China's primary need was to use all its resources and men to reconstruct the country following eleven years of war (the world war and its own civil war). It was a huge human sacrifice: about one million Chinese soldiers were killed. The war ended, not with a peace treaty, but with a mere armistice (a stopping of the war) in 1953. Nearly seventy years later, the war was technically still ongoing.

Beginning in 1957 and into the early 1970s, Great Britain's colonies in Asia, Africa, and Polynesia won their independence. In 1922 the empire contained more than 458 million people—20 percent of the world's population—in a territory of 13 million square miles—25 percent of the earth's territory. Between 1945 and 1965, the number of people under British rule dropped from 700 million to 5 million, with 3 million of those living in Hong Kong. In the decolonization of the British Empire, most colonies peacefully gained their independence. But there

As a Korean War corpsman methodically and unemotionally fills out casualty tags, a twenty-year-old American soldier is comforted by the first sergeant: the body of his buddy had just been carried to this point from the mountain on which he was killed. Ironically, the sergeant was killed a few days later. National Archives 531370

were two—Malaya and Kenya—that experienced the throes of violent colonial resistance beforehand.

Britain had been active in Malayan political life since the eighteenth century, but Malaya was not a unitary state, instead made up of a variety of state units that created complicated relationships with Britain over time. Malaya was ethnically divided: the Malays were its original people; however, in the development of its two major industries, tin and rubber, Chinese and Indian laborers moved or were brought in. In its colonial rule (late 1700s to 1957), Britain played the same "divide and rule" card it opted for in India. It developed policies that favored the Malays, whose sultans were Britain's initial contacts and first allies, and it discriminated against ethnic Chinese and Indians. The British constantly appeased the Malays, careful that they did not antagonize them as Malay nationalism grew in the 1940s. Chinese and Indian residents were denied the right to vote, had no land rights, and were excluded from participating in governmental administration. In 1946, Britain proposed the establishment of the Malayan Union, where all citizens—Malays, Chinese, and Indian—would have equal rights. The Malays rejected this and briefly boycotted serving in any sort of governmental position. The British gave in to the Malays, and in 1948, they set up the Federation of Malaya (or Malaysia) that protected all the rights and privileges of the Malays, leaving the Chinese and the Indians to fend for themselves.

In 1948, an ethnic Chinese guerrilla insurgency broke out under the flag of the Communist Party of Malaya to overthrow the British. The catalyst for the action was the British cancellation of the Malayan Union, which took away any chance the non-Malays would get equal rights; the Chinese were especially infuriated because they had been more heavily involved than other ethnic groups in resisting and fighting the Japanese. Adding injury to insult, from June 1948 through April 1950, the British deported thirty-five thousand Chinese to Hong Kong, accusing them of being part of the guerrilla action. As a mark of the reality of decolonization, the British, wanting to keep their colony, called the insurgency the Malayan Emergency; the communists called it the Anti-British National Liberation War.

In many ways, the insurgency was a prelude of sorts of aspects of the later American war in Vietnam. For the Chinese guerrillas, it was a war of intimidation, sabotage, ambushes, and selective assassinations. The British met fire with fire. They routinely beat up Chinese squatters when they refused to give information about the guerrillas. In the field, they practiced decapitation and mutilation, destroyed tens of thousands of homes, burned hundreds of villages, and booby-trapped jungle food storages. They created 450 "new villages" where they forcibly resettled 500,000 Chinese; these were actually prison camps where they tortured and beat people almost incessantly. In addition, their practices included spraying the herbicide (chemical toxin) Agent Orange, undertaking saturation bombing, and adopting the strategy of "search and destroy." In 1957, Malaysia won its independence peacefully; although the rebellion continued until 1960, it had lost its anticolonial purpose. In those twelve years, about 6,700 guerrillas were killed, close to 1,800 Malayan and Commonwealth troops, and more than 3,000 civilians.

The British in Kenya seemed to be replaying the role of Germans in their colony in Southwest Africa from 1904 to 1907. As the Germans were to the Herero and Nama in Namibia, so were the British to the Kikuyo in Kenya. The appalling abuse (physical and psychological torture) forced on the largest tribe, the Kikuyu, was designed to preserve the British settler system of racist and economic privilege. But for the Mau Mau participants, their reaction to economic emptiness and deprivation came ultimately because of the greater losses of land to white British settlers. Like the Germans, the British settlers' goal was to seize the land of the natives for themselves and to turn all natives into the settlers' wage laborers. As with the Germans in Namibia, life in Kenya became a zero-sum game with the British always building a sum and the Kikuyu piling up zeros.[4]

In a book about his uncle who was killed in the Mau Mau uprising that began in 1952, human rights activist Koigi Wa Wamwere spelled out the roots of the insurgency: land, which was their link to "eternal existence."

> For the Africans, land meant more to them than food and a house. It was their permanent residence, during and after life. To fight for land and freedom, Mau Mau was trying to secure their eternal existence. Refusing to understand this, the British subjected them to great misrepresentation. They called them *itoi* (rebels), *imaramari* (terrorists), *washenzi* (primitive people), as well as atavistic, cannibalistic, and beastly. [The British said that the Mau Mau] were fighting [not for land and freedom but] to return to a past of primitiveness, darkness, death, and evil.[5]

In the insurrection, the goal of the Kikuyu and other participating Kenyans was to overthrow the British and establish an independent nation-state. Mau Mau leaders were relatively well educated; they fought using guerrilla tactics, mainly with night attacks on settlers or British officials, and women maintained supply lines. The British reaction to the uprising was horror and outrage at such brazen native impudence; one European psychiatrist ignorantly posited to white Kenyans that the Mau Mau were "an irrational force of evil, dominated by bestial impulses, and influenced by world communism."[6]

For their part in putting down the insurrection, the British forcibly placed 1.2 to 1.5 million Kikuyus into "enclosed villages" (a system of camps known as "the Pipeline")[7] where men were castrated, burned alive, anally raped, flogged, and starved; women suffered having their breasts cut off with pliers, sodomization, and rape. In addition, anti-insurgency tactics included summary executions, electric shock, mass killings, slave labor, burning down of villages, and soaking prisoners with human waste.[8] Tens of thousands were tortured to get them to renounce their oath to the Mau Mau. More than 1,090 men were hanged, the most lopsided use of capital punishment in the empire, doubling the number the French executed in Algeria. Later it was discovered that almost half of those executed were not in fact Mau Mau rebels.

One detainee was future US president Barack Obama's grandfather; British soldiers forced pins under his fingernails and into his buttocks, squeezing his testicles between metal rods. The government officially reported that 11,000 Mau Mau were killed. A general estimate, however, is that at least 25,000 rebels died; it has been suggested that deaths due to acts of cruelty may have reached 300,000, almost thirty times the mainstream figure of 11,000. Two hundred British soldiers died, and thirty-two white settlers were killed. Equally shocking was the lying and "covering up" by key British leaders about the truth—right up through Prime Minister Winston Churchill (1951–55) and his successors, Anthony Eden (1955–57) and Harold Macmillan (1957–63).[9]

In the late 1940s and in the early 1950s, both the economy and politics in France and Italy were in dangerous disarray. Both had to deal with postwar reconstruction, and both had distinctly damaging high rates of inflation. In Italy a Parliamentary Commission on Poverty published in 1953 its dismaying findings: 24 percent of Italian families were destitute or "in hardship," 21 percent of dwellings were overcrowded, 52 percent of homes in the south had no running drinking water, and only 57 percent of homes had an indoor toilet. Politically, the Italians had to deal with two serious problems: the fate of the monarchy and the reality of a perceived communist threat. In 1947, Italy had the largest Communist Party in Europe with 2.3 million members. The Communist Party was the main opposition to the ruling Christian Democrats, but in the 1948 election, the socialist and communist parties joined together in the Popular Democratic Front, certain that the votes for both parties would outnumber those for the Christian Democrats. In the 1948 election campaign, a worried and fearful United States became deeply involved, even using CIA operatives, to help defeat the leftists.[10] In France, in addition to the serious economic problems were the white-hot memories of the cringe-worthy scandal of Petain's Vichy regime and the bitter reality that roughly ten thousand French were executed as Nazi collaborators. After elections in October 1945, the French Communist Party held 30 percent of the seats in the National Assembly, more than doubling its number from the 1936 election.

Fearful that communists in France and Italy might seize control of their governments, the United States launched the Marshall Plan, providing large loans and grants (in the sum of US$15 billion) to make Europe's recovery more rapid and certain. Aid went to sixteen Western

European nations, including West Germany, Britain, France (these three received the most aid), Belgium, the Netherlands, Norway, Italy, and Switzerland. The program was clearly successful: the countries involved saw a rise in GNP (gross national product) of 15 to 25 percent in these years. This assistance was crucial in giving support and substantial renewal to the chemical, engineering, and steel industries.

Because France was threatened in so many ways at home, Paris was desperate to retain its overseas empire in Southeast Asia, Africa, and Oceania. They had established their overbearing and brutal control of Indochina (Cambodia, Laos, and Vietnam) beginning in the 1860s. Since the 1910s, the Vietnamese had looked for a way to throw off the French yoke; in 1941, nationalist Ho Chi Minh organized the Vietminh (League for the Independence of Vietnam). At the end of World War II in August 1945, he declared the establishment of the Democratic Republic of Vietnam as an independent nation, but the French were determined to smash it and restore French empire through war (1946–1954). Ho and the Vietminh fought to finally achieve national unity and independence. But the United States, continuing to look through its Cold War lenses, was blinded by its own paranoia; by 1954, it was paying 78 percent of the war costs for the French. The French defeat at the Battle of Dienbienphu in May 1954 ended its empire in Southeast Asia. Panicked by the French defeat, the United States offered to give the French nuclear weapons; that proposed deal was not consummated. So then the United States took up the cause itself, sending first advisors to Vietnam in the early 1960s, then the first Marine units in March 1965.

After the years of the French conquest of Algeria (1830–1847), settlers immigrated in large numbers from France, Italy, and Spain to Algiers and beyond. In 1848, Algeria became a French department, one of the three administrative levels of government below the national level. A century later, in 1954, it was home to a million settlers (10 percent of the population). In the process, the French destroyed Muslim villages, desecrated Muslim mosques, stole Arab land, and forced Muslims to move to make room for European farms and industries. A century of discrimination against the Muslim majority stimulated a fervent nationalism. The Algerian War for independence erupted in November 1954 with bombings by the Front de Liberation Nationale (FLN). Frantz Fanon, a member of the FLN wrote about the nature of the war between colonizer and colonized: "Terror, counter-terror, violence, counter-violence: that is what observers bitterly record when they describe the circle of hate, which is so *tenacious* and so evident in

Algeria."[11] Brutally marked by terror and torture on both sides, the war ended in 1962 with Algerian independence.

Fanon was an Afro-Caribbean Martinique-born psychiatrist whose interest focused on the psychology of colonization and decolonization. In 1952, he published *Black Skin, White Masks*, a study of the psychopathology of the colonial subjugation of blacks. Fanon noted one consistent psychic difficulty of the colonized: "The oppressed will always believe the worst about themselves." In *The Wretched of the Earth* (1961), he argued that a colonized people could use violence to gain their independence because they, not thought to be fully human by their colonizers, were not bound by any consideration of the "humanity" of the colonizers. Through his life and his works as a Marxist existentialist, he inspired movements of national liberation in the Middle East, Africa, Asia, and even the United States. Despite being overthrown by wars of national liberation, imperialism, Fanon said, "leaves behind germs of rot which we must clinically detect and remove from our land but from our minds as well."[12] That was the continuing work of decolonization.

Concurrent with decolonization efforts and their frequent racial overtones were two diametrically opposed racial programs being played out in the United States and South Africa. In the US civil rights movement, blacks waged a struggle with whites for their rights and proper place in society in the 1950s and 1960s. Despite school desegregation in the mid-1950s, discriminatory laws and practices, especially in the South, continued. The act igniting the civil rights movement was the 1955 refusal of Rosa Parks, a seamstress at a Montgomery, Alabama, department store, to change her seat at the front of a public bus to accommodate a white rider. At the time of her arrest, she was secretary of the local branch of the National Association for the Advancement of Colored People (NAACP), an advocacy organization established in 1909. She explained her actions: "People always say that I didn't give up my seat because I was tired, but that isn't true. . . No, the only tired I was, was tired of giving in." Her arrest touched off a 381-day boycott of Montgomery buses, led by a local pastor, Martin Luther King Jr., who became the movement's principal leader.

Dancer, singer, actress, and activist in the French Resistance, Josephine Baker assiduously supported the American civil rights movement in the 1950s. Though based in France, she traveled to the United States frequently and worked with the NAACP. She was with Dr. King at one of his key career moments—his "I Have a Dream" speech at the March on Washington for Jobs and Freedom on August 28, 1963. Dressed in her French Resistance uniform, Baker was the only official

Perhaps Martin Luther King Jr.'s most illustrious day was August 28, 1963, when he gave his eloquent "I Have a Dream" speech at the Lincoln Memorial. The rally at the memorial was the culmination of the March on Washington for Jobs and Freedom, attended by an estimated 250,000 people. Photo by Central Press/Getty 2674125

female speaker. In her speech, right before MLK spoke on November 28, 1963, she compared her positive life in France as a black woman to her experiences in the United States.

> When I got to New York, . . . they would not let me check into the good hotels because I was colored, or eat in certain restaurants. . . . I have walked into the palaces of kings . . . and into the houses of presidents. But I could not walk into a hotel in America and get a cup of coffee, and that made me mad . . . and when I demanded what I was supposed to have and what I was entitled to, they still would not give it to me. . . . They thought they could smear me, and the best way to do that was to call me a communist . . . [a] dreaded word in those days. . . . But they . . . were mad because I told the truth.[13]

In the aftermath of the March on Washington, the US civil rights movement had notable legislative successes with the passage of laws eliminating legal barriers in voting and ending discrimination in employment practices and public accommodations.

In contrast, the white South African government was boxing its blacks into a stifling system of apartheid (apartness). Opposing apartheid was the largest black organization in South Africa, the African National Congress (ANC) founded in 1912. In 1950 the Group Areas Act formally segregated the races. The ANC responded with a campaign of civil disobedience led by lawyer Nelson Mandela. A 1951 act re-established tribal organizations for black Africans and created ten homelands, or Bantustans, where blacks had to live. Mandela and others led the ANC in a Defiance Campaign; more than 8,500, including Mandela, were arrested for defying apartheid laws. The 1953 Bantu Education Act segregated schools with the goal of shunting blacks to poorer schools and ultimately to unskilled labor markets. The Afrikaner government spent 90 percent of its education budget on white schools and only 10 percent on black schools.

Minister of Native Affairs Hendrik Verwoerd, the "architect of apartheid," pontificated: "There is no place for the [Bantu] in the European community above the level of certain forms of labor. . . . What is the use of teaching mathematics when it cannot use it in practice."[14] The racism implicit in Verwoerd's use of "it" in referring to a black person revealed apartheid's foundations. Violent racial incidents became increasingly common. In 1959, police in Durban were involved in a melee clubbing local women who were upset because of police entering their homes to stop home-brewing alcohol. The women brewed so their men would drink at home and not pay high prices for drinks at a new local brew hall. The melee was preceded by women setting fire to the new brewery. The episode reflected racial misunderstandings and lack of effective communication. Regarding the movement of blacks, the state required blacks over sixteen to carry passbooks (like internal passports) wherever they went. In March 1960, demonstrations against the "pass laws" led to a police massacre of sixty-nine people in Sharpsville township. In a June 1964 trial, Mandela was sentenced to life imprisonment for plotting sabotage against the government.

At a time when decolonization had generally become the global trend, imperialism could still rear its ugly head. Britain had controlled Egypt via a protectorate, especially over its foreign and defense policies, from 1882 until 1952. In that latter year, Arab nationalist Gamal Abdul Nasser, who, as a youth, had demonstrated against British control, led a coup that toppled the Egyptian monarchy. In September 1955, Egypt acted to cut Israel off from its only outlet to the Indian Ocean by closing the Strait of Tiran at the mouth of the Gulf of Aqaba between the Sinai Peninsula and Saudi Arabia. Israel was ready to fight to reopen the

Apartheid government efforts to evict blacks from an enclave peopled largely by blacks and Indians and forcibly move them to a newly established black township on the city's outskirts led on June 16, 1959, to feminine rioting and violent resistance. Three days later, still embittered and furiously angry, women met in Durban and were challenged and beaten by police. AP Photo 6204170218

strait since Egypt had refused Israel the right to use the Suez Canal. Then a crisis suddenly arose over the canal, built in the nineteenth century by a joint British-French company, which still administered it. The United States and Britain precipitated the crisis by withdrawing promised funding for the Aswan Dam, which was crucial for Egypt's own development goals. In response, on July 26, 1956, Nasser nationalized the canal, seizing it from the French and the British to provide funding for the construction of the Aswan Dam. Nationalization was not illegal, and Nasser promised to buy out shareholders completely and to ensure that transportation on the canal would not be disrupted.

Britain and France saw in Nasser's defiance a huge blow to their prestige and political standing in northern Africa and the Middle East; for all European colonizers, defiance on the part of the colonized could not be tolerated. So, from the British perspective, here was one of their protectorate's lackeys challenging his country's recent overlord: Did Nasser not know his place in the world order? The British and the French negotiated with Israel to start a war in which they hoped to take the canal back. Israel invaded Sinai and Anglo-French troops invaded the Suez Canal zone, but international and domestic reactions were so strongly negative that they were forced to back down in eight days. British opinion was polarized between those who still wanted to uphold prestige through imperialism and those who saw imperialism as squalid and impossible to countenance at that late date. Israel left the Sinai and the Gaza Strip in March 1957, withdrawing in exchange for the stationing of UN peacekeepers to secure the Israeli-Egyptian border and to maintain free passage to the Indian Ocean. For Egypt and Nasser, the outcome was a triumph: he had successfully defied arrogant Western imperialists.

The 1950s was a period of reconstruction from the war and in the West a longing for prewar cultural and social normalcy. Many yearned for "the good life," which usually meant more income and leisure. In the Western world and Japan, television became the supplier of mass culture, with 56 million sets in the United States, over 11 million in the United Kingdom, and 6 million in Japan in 1960.[15] As a backlash against the bland social normalcy of the 1950s, many alienated intellectuals protested the cultural ethos and the hypocrisy of American society. The core of Beat Generation writers were literary iconoclasts and strongly individualistic against the social, political, and cultural forces that would rein them in and enforce obedience, acquiescence, conventionality, docility, and submission.

Jack Kerouac's *On the Road* (1957) and other writings focused on the topics of Catholic spirituality, jazz, promiscuity, Buddhism, drugs, poverty, and travel.[16] Allen Ginsberg's most well-known work is the long poem *Howl*, published in 1956. In it Ginsberg denounces the deadly forces in the United States of both capitalism and conformity. The first lines in *Howl* emphasize the importance of drugs for the Beat population: "I saw the best minds of my generation destroyed by madness, starving hysterical naked, dragging themselves through the negro streets at dawn looking for an angry fix."[17] William S. Burroughs in *Naked Lunch* (1959) continued the themes of Kerouac and Ginsberg.[18] His is a dark picture of the horrors of heroin addiction and withdrawal from it. The novel is a wild dream of paranoia, erotica, and drug-induced hallucinations.

All three participated essentially in a transnational critique: intellectuals in countries around the globe embraced, on their own or after contact with the American Beats, the Beat mission of challenging political, social, and cultural forces that normalized conformity. These powerful stimuli had the potential to dictate people's place in society and compel actions that, in effect, would stultify and paralyze their lives. Echoing the thoughts of Lu Xun and Garcia Lorca in the 1930s about the individual's role in taking on tyrannical forces, Czech playwright Vaclav Havel argued that Beat literature was "a potential instrument for resistance to the totalitarian system that had been imposed on our existence."[19] An example of cultural globalization, the Beat ethos made its mark in Morocco, Japan, India, European nations, Canada, Mexico, Cuba, Nicaragua, and Peru. Though the seeds were sown in the 1950s, some of these Beat movements emerged only in the late 1960s or later.

The 1950s saw the advent of rock and roll, in the beginning a combination of rhythm and blues, gospel, country, jazz, and boogie-woogie piano, which grew from the increasing contact between blacks and whites. While the music conveyed youthful aimlessness and angst, its vulgarity and sexual connotations frightened parents who actually believed that it caused juvenile delinquency. It was crooner Frank Sinatra's over-the-top screed on the genre that summed up the older generations' views: "Rock and Roll is lewd, sly, in plain fact, dirty—a rancid-smelling aphrodisiac and the martial music of every side-burned delinquent on the face of the earth."[20]

The "king of rock and roll" and one of the social, cultural, and pop-figure icons of the twentieth century was Elvis Presley. Born and raised in the American South, he, like many white rock stars, was much influenced by African American styles, which he incorporated into his music. One of the most acclaimed singers of the twentieth century, Presley remains the highest-selling solo musician in the history of recorded music. Presley was a global phenomenon: 40 percent of the sales from his records and CDs came from outside the US: primarily Western European nations as well as Japan, Australia, South Africa, and Canada. In Russia, Presley's music did not become a hit until twenty-five years after his death in 1977; the first CD of his music was released in 2002. Fan clubs, some developing thirty or forty years after his death, as well as festivals celebrating his music, continued to be international phenomena. The Tokyo Elvis Presley Fan Club in 2002 had about five thousand members. Tens of thousands from around the globe attend the annual Tupelo Elvis Festival in Presley's Mississippi hometown. At the 2012 festival, a seven-foot bronze statue of the "King" was unveiled as the mayor intoned the words, "This is hallowed ground."

The other international rock stars of the 1960s were the Beatles, whose world tour in 1964 touched off almost worshipful hysteria among their ardent fans and led to their global stardom. Originally calling themselves the Beetles, they changed the spelling to Beatles, reportedly to put them squarely in line with the Beat generation. They combined country, blues, and pop (like Elvis) but also added music hall and Broadway to their sound. Relentlessly imaginative and experimental, the Beatles captured and held international mass consciousness well past their 1970 breakup. Their supremacy as rock icons remains unchallenged to this day.

The Beat generation, Elvis Presley, and the Beatles were all searching for something to give more meaning to their lives. For the Beat poets, two elements that emerged as cultural goals were "making a spiritual quest" and "exploring American and Eastern religions." Elvis was reportedly fascinated by all the world's religions or religious views; he treated them as if they were some kind of thought buffet through which he could choose his own personalized religious package: Hinduism, Judaism, Christianity, numerology, theosophy, mind control, and positive thinking. It is noteworthy, that like the Beat poets, Presley specifically

Guys, Guys, Guys!!! This is my favorite band!!! Just wanted to share to the next owner of this textbook ☺

The music of the Beatles transformed the world of rock and roll; they were international stars from 1964 until their breakup in 1970. Left to right are John Lennon, Paul McCartney, and George Harrison. Seated at the drums is Ringo Starr. Library of Congress, LC-USZ62-122935

included Western and Eastern religions. In that religious vein, it is perhaps surprising that, though he was the "king" of rock and roll, the only two Grammy Awards that he won were for gospel songs ("How Great Thou Art" and "He Touched Me"). Gospel songs grew out of oral traditions of black evangelical churches in the southern United States.

The Beatles had grown up in standard Christian denominations, but, before they had formed their band, they had dropped religious practices altogether. Yet they continued to hope and search for some higher purpose in their lives. John Lennon noted that the "Beatles made it, stopped touring, and had all the money and fame they wanted and found out—they had nothing." Or again, "It's the odd bit about money, power, and fame not being the answer."[21] Paul McCartney put it this way in a 1969 interview: "We were looking for something; we'd been into drugs, and the next step was finding a meaning for it all."[22]

In 1968, the Beatles and their retinue traveled to Rishikesh, India, to study transcendental meditation (TM) with Maharishi Mahesh Yogi, the founder of the spiritual regeneration movement. The year before, they attended a conference in Wales, where the Maharishi lectured on transcendental meditation. At that conference, they announced, in their search for new higher values, that they were giving up drugs. Their trip to India was to study to become TM instructors. In speaking of TM, George Harrison, the Beatle most excited by this venture, argued that "everything else can wait, but the search for God cannot wait."[23] Lennon described a young woman studying at the Indian center who spent the most of her time in meditation; he concluded that the woman "was trying to find God quicker than anyone else."[24]

In the 1960s and beyond, TM went global. At the turn of the twenty-first century, 114 countries around the world had TM centers; the United States had more than 370 such centers. The country with the largest percentage of participants was Israel, with 50,000 people who been trained in TM. Overall estimates of people around the world who studied TM reached 900,000 in 1970; 1 million by 1980; and 4 to 10 million in the early twenty-first century. But, in terms of world religions, TM had only a relatively small number of participants compared to, say, Roman Catholic Church members.

Catholicism is a global religion: in 2013, there were 1.2 billion Catholics, 16.8 percent of the world's population. In January 1959, Pope John XXIII launched a revolutionary movement that changed the face of worship procedures. He summoned the Second Vatican Council to update Catholic practices for its worship and work in the modern world; it met during autumns from 1962 through 1965. Both Pope John

XXIII (who died in 1963) and his successor Paul VI made clear that the Council would change processes and procedures, but it would make no changes in Church doctrine.

The role of women in the Church was a major issue; the Council decided that women could participate in the leadership of the mass, taking on such roles as readers, Eucharistic ministers, and sometimes altar servers. Despite allowing women to play a more conspicuous role in the mass, Paul VI essentially upheld the idea that women's proper roles were as mother and housewife. In his address to women on the last day of the Council, he declared, "You women have always had as your lot the protection of the home, the love of beginnings, and an understanding of cradles."[25] The most decisive change brought by Vatican II was that mass would be conducted in the language of the people, not in Latin, opening up worship in a new way.

The Vatican Council also addressed questions about relations between the Church and non-Christian religions. In a 1965 declaration "In Our Time," the Church called for working together with Hindus, Buddhists, Muslims, and Jews for mutual understanding and benefit. Perhaps its stance on Judaism was the Council's greatest theological step forward: that Jews were not responsible for killing Jesus, that Jews be thought of not as the other but as children of the same God. In that light, the Church agreed to an ongoing dialogue with Jews. It also no longer prohibited Catholics' attending Protestant services or reading from a Protestant Bible. It still declared, however, that the Roman Catholic Church was the true church. Pope John XXIII was canonized by Pope Francis on April 21, 2014, as a saint "of courage and mercy who responded to challenges of [his] time by modernizing the Catholic Church in fidelity to its ancient traditions" and "who helped bring the church to the people."[26]

CHAPTER 5

Struggling for Equality, Freedom, and Peace, 1966–1979

The counterculture of the late 1960s and 1970s was built on rock music, psychedelic drugs, alternative life styles, and sexual exploration. Huge rock concerts marked these years, including the 1969 Woodstock and the Altamont Free Concert (which was studded with violence) in the United States; the 1970 Isle of Wight Festival, the largest of all time, with a total audience of at least 600,000 people; and the 1973 Summer Jam at Watkins Glen, New York. Their lifestyle of partying notwithstanding, hippies and other protestors saw the world as grim and out of control, run by military and bureaucratic elites and marked by wars, rebellions, coups, assassinations, and genocide—with deaths numbering in the millions. The tongue-in-cheek observation by Abbie Hoffman, a hippie involved in protests at the 1968 Democratic National Convention in Chicago, contained more than a grain of truth for this period: "I believe in compulsory cannibalism. If people were forced to eat what they killed, there would be no more wars."[1]

The counterculture championed protest: anti-war, anti-establishment, anti-conventional. It tackled racial, feminist, and gay issues, advocating civil rights for all. But ironically, the struggles for equality, freedom, and peace sometimes gave rise to violence. Mass student protests erupted in the United States, France, Czechoslovakia, West Germany, England, Sweden, Spain, Italy, Mexico, Brazil, Jamaica, Australia, and Japan—about student living conditions, university costs, and the current political situations in those countries.

Apartheid in South Africa continued its bleak march. During the 1970s more than three million blacks were forcibly "resettled" in black homelands. Because of apartheid, South Africa was embargoed, isolated, and prohibited from participating in the United Nations, in the Olympic

The Twentieth Century: A World History. Keith Schoppa, Oxford University Press. © Oxford University Press 2021.
DOI: 10.1093/oso/9780190497354.003.0006

Games from 1964 to 1988, in world sporting events, and in global and regional cultural associations. Bombings of trains, railroad stations and track, police stations, and oil refineries punctuated the 1970s. Stephen (Steve) Biko, son of a government clerk and a domestic worker in white homes, was an anti-apartheid activist. In 1968, Biko founded and served as first president of the South African Students' Organization (SASO), an organization for black, Indian, and "coloured" students. In these years, he developed the Black Consciousness Movement (BCM). Through his writings and activism, he aimed to empower blacks, arguing for two steps in developing black consciousness: psychological liberation and physical liberation, concepts that he shared with Frantz Fanon. His slogan, "Black is beautiful," meant essentially, "Man, you are OK as you are; begin to look upon yourself as a human being." Biko wrote, "Being black is not a matter of pigmentation—being black is a reflection of a mental attitude."[2]

Biko's thought and leadership did much to inspire the Soweto Uprising in June 1976. The state had decided that math, arithmetic, and social studies high school courses had to be taught in Afrikaans, a dialect spoken by early Dutch settlers that students considered "the language of the oppressor." Between 10,000 and 20,000 black students walked out of their schools to attend a rally at Orlando City Stadium; as they walked, police opened fire on the defenseless students, gunning down 176. In other student demonstrations across the country, at least 600 were killed. From the time of the Soweto massacre, black resistance mushroomed.

In late August 1977, Biko was arrested at a police roadblock. Interrogated, tortured, and beaten, he sank into a coma from massive head injuries. On September 11, he was loaded into the back of a Land Rover, unconscious, naked, with manacled hands and ankles, and driven seven hundred miles to Pretoria. Just after arriving, he died from a brain hemorrhage. His murder was never prosecuted. Outrage swept the globe with a sense that something must be done to South Africa. With full support from the West, the UN Security Council imposed a mandatory arms embargo. Nelson Mandela, later the first black South African president, wrote, "Steve lives on in the galaxy of brave and courageous leaders who helped shape democratic South Africa."[3]

Civil rights efforts in the United States had already borne considerable fruit by the late 1960s, yet there were problems evidenced by destructive black riots in major cities every summer from 1964 to 1967, with loss of life and property mostly in black communities. The assassination of Martin Luther King Jr. in April 1968 was followed by a tsunami of violent insurrections in cities nationwide. Without King, who would head the civil rights movement? King's wife, Coretta Scott King, approached Josephine Baker about taking her husband's place as head of the American civil rights movement; Baker demurred because of her twelve young adopted children.

Well before his death, King and his nonviolent strategy had been challenged by some who contended that white America would never allow blacks to participate fully in American life. They believed that blacks had to take charge of their own lives, setting up institutions that would serve blacks and provide a sense of "Black Power" and consciousness in organizations like the Black Panthers. By the mid-1970s, the civil rights movement had melted into the background, as the government strategy, so constructive in the 1960s, became, in the words of Richard Nixon, one of "benign neglect."

In this period women worked to expand their own civil rights. One of the most important texts serving the thought of women pursuing feminist goals was Simone de Beauvoir's 1949 book, *The Second Sex*. De Beauvoir was a Parisian existentialist philosopher, whose doctoral degree in philosophy from the Sorbonne was only the ninth such degree that women had received from that institution. She chose to teach at the lycée (high school) level from 1929 to 1943. At the beginning of her teaching, she and Jean-Paul Sartre, an existentialist philosopher, who also chose to teach at several lycée, became a couple, though they never married.

She began her discussion of feminism focusing on patriarchal control and the male perspective that had developed in the ancient world of hunters and gatherers, which had oppressed women. As things are, she wrote, "He is the Subject . . . the Absolute. She is 'the Other'—and that identity is at base the source of women's oppression." Or, again, "Humanity is male, and man defines woman, not in herself but in relation to himself. She is not considered an autonomous being."[4] As an existentialist, she contended that existence preceded essence; thus, one is not born a woman, but becomes one. She understood freedom as a universal—meaning that each project humans undertake "requires the achievement of freedom."[5] Women, like men, could choose to elevate themselves from the state of "stagnation" to that of "transcendence," from which they could work on projects that opened up freedom for themselves.

One of women's practical concerns about freedom and achievement was how their year-round, full-time wages compared to men's. From 1951 to 1960 American women generally received about 64.0

cents per dollar earned by men. However, in both the 1960s and 1970s, women's wages dropped below the 60.0-cents-per-dollar level—to as low as 57.0 cents per dollar. From 1980 to 1990 women received 60.2 to 71.6 cents per dollar earned by men. Women's salary compared to men's grew much more slowly from 1990 to 2000 (from 71.6 cents up to 73.7) and from 2000 to 2009 (from 73.7 cents to 77.0 cents); so, from 1990 for almost two decades, to 2009, women's salary vis-à-vis men's increased 5.4 cents. Statistics from 2018 break down the racial/national backgrounds of the women: whites, 79.0 cents; blacks, 62.0 cents; Hispanics, 54.0 cents; Asians, 90.0 cents; and American Indians and Alaskans, 67.0 cents. Since 2018, however, no progress was made on closing the gender pay gap further.[6] Although there were few highpoints in the realm of women's salary (Australia did order equal pay for women in 1972), women continued to break through in important governmental positions: as prime ministers in India, Indira Gandhi (1966); in Israel, Golda Meir (1968); and in the United

Golda Meir, a Zionist from the 1920s on, visits a kibbutz in January 1971. Though she was a dominating, contentious, inflexible, and uncompromising leader, Meir was also a dauntless and conscientious woman with a refreshingly total absence of pretense. These qualities were critical to her strong leadership in the Yom Kippur War of 1973, which Israel won after a very shaky start. Government Press Office (Israel)

Kingdom, Margaret Thatcher (1979); and as president in Argentina, Isabel Perón (1974).

Gender equity of female and male athletes at the Summer Olympics provides one marker to the growing involvement of women in significant global events. At the 1900 Games, 2 percent of the 997 competitors were women. It took until the 1976 Games for women's participation to rise above 20 percent (20.7). In 2000, women made up 38 percent of the 10,651 competitors. In 2016, female participants had continued their slow climb to 45 percent. The Winter Games showed roughly the same gender differentiation. In short, women have made great progress in this arena, but in the minds of many, there was still more to achieve.

The UN General Assembly declared 1975 to be the International Women's Year and organized the official World Conference on Women held in Mexico City (1979); all participants were governmental representatives. A most important outcome of this conference was its adoption of the first human rights treaty to uphold the reproductive rights of women. There was a parallel conference in Mexico City, the International Women's Year Tribune. The US delegation to the tribune convention was headed by two leading US feminists: Betty Friedan, author of the 1963 book *The Feminist Critique*, in which she diagnosed midcentury women's general unhappiness as depression because they were forced to be subservient to men financially, mentally, physically, and intellectually; and Gloria Steinem, author of seventy-two books, including *Outrageous Acts and Everyday Rebellions* (1983), in which she discussed a variety of important feminist issues.

There was a "divide" at this conference between women from developed countries and those from developing countries. Whereas women from developed societies wanted to stress individual freedom, those from developing, socialist, or communist states wanted to talk about the state's obligation to enforce the collective rights of all members of society. When discussing specific problems, the latter group of women related how technology from the developed world often displaced women who had been practicing subsistence agriculture; often, their path afterward was working in industries where they were exploited as cheap labor.

Women from the developed world wanted to talk about issues of gender equality and about sexual and reproductive health and rights. They were met, however, by women who were determined to focus on survival and more pressing issues, arguing that women's problems could never be separated from their political and economic contexts. It was a passionate disagreement—no one minced words.[7] The socialist and communist delegates mocked American feminists "as spoiled bourgeois elites raising marginal concerns to avoid confronting more pressing issues of racism, imperialism, colonialism, and poverty."[8] Even though it was International Women's Year, the outlooks of the women around the globe remained uncomfortably at odds.

Other minorities that began human rights struggles in the late 1960s and 1970s were gay, bisexual, and transgender people. Discriminated against and frequently humiliated, beaten, and arrested, homosexuals were often the victims of police raids on bars. On June 28, 1969, the police raided a New York City bar, the Stonewall Inn, to close it; it had a primarily homosexual clientele, almost completely male and racially mixed. The raid ignited a riot by the gay community, and it continued for several days. Outrage at the police action spread, and the straight community was moved to join in the demonstrations. It was the first such spontaneous violent resistance to the police.

In Mexico City, 1975, there were two parallel women's conferences: the official UN gathering of government representatives, and the so-called Tribune, a nongovernmental conference. While the UN conference maintained its "official" ambiance, women demonstrated outside the Tribune conference, where there was lively debate about the roles of women, especially between women from developed countries and those from developing, socialist, and communist countries. UN Photo 122986

The Gay Liberation Front (GLF) was founded in the aftermath of the riots. By 1971, the GLF and other gay rights organizations were in all major American cities, three countries in the British Commonwealth, and in four countries in Western Europe. The manifesto of the GLF published in London in 1971 argued that

> gay people are oppressed. . . . We face the prejudice, hostility and vio-
> lence of straight society, and the opportunities open to us in work and
> leisure are restricted. . . . Shouldn't we demand reforms that will give
> us tolerance and equality? Certainly we should. . . .They are our civil
> rights. . . . [But] we do not intend to ask for anything. We intend to
> stand firm and assert our basic rights. If this involves violence, it will
> not be we who initiate this, but those who attempt to stand in our way
> to freedom.[9]

In 1973, the American Psychiatric Association voted unanimously to declassify homosexuality as a mental illness. In 1975, the American Medical Association called for repeal of all state laws prohibiting homosexual acts between consenting adults. In Muslim and some Asian countries, by contrast, attaining gay rights was rare indeed: same-sex relationships were punishable by death in some Mideast and African countries. Gay rights came to Asia (Israel) and Africa (South Africa) only in the 1980s and 1990s. Most countries in the Middle East, Africa, and western Asia have severe penalties for same-sex contact. When Great Britain oversaw its decolonization, it seemed to offer its liberal hand to foster such connections. But, as of 2018, more than half of the seventy-one countries that criminalized homosexuality were former British colonies and protectorates.

The American civil rights movement reverberated around the world and served as a model and inspiration for some minorities. Other models included individual people—King, Gandhi, Biko, Mandela, and, for some in the Middle East, Nasser. The Northern Ireland Civil Rights Association, founded to end the sectarian discrimination of the Protestants against the Catholics, consciously modeled itself on the American efforts. Quebec Canada's Quiet Revolution (1960–1966) brought large-scale rejection of past values (agriculturalism, where rural life had been the acceptable model for a modernizing system; anti-statism; and messianism, belief among the people of Quebec that their particular cause was destined to triumph). The Quiet Revolution entered a phase of modernization where outlooks became increasingly more liberal, more secular, and more democratic; and where laws were enacted to establish a social safety net and to make education and social services accessible to all. In the end, the Quiet Revolution fueled the Quebec Sovereignty movement. Meanwhile, Czechoslovakia had its "Prague Spring," a brief period of liberalization under Alexander Dubcek in 1968, ending with the Warsaw Pact invasion of the country.

The Soviet Union saw a movement for civil and human rights from the 1960s to the 1980s, where groups ranging from youth activists to academics, like Andre Sakharov, sought freedom of expression and conscience, freedom to emigrate, and asserted their concerns over the plight of political prisoners. The key word was "freedom." Their approach was characterized by a new openness to dissent and focused on legality and process. They expressed their dissent through individual and group protest letters and petitions, documenting repression and rights violations in the unsanctioned press, and unauthorized demonstrations. The dissent came with great risk: dismissal from work or studies; deportation to labor camps; and hospitalization for "punitive psychiatry," where dissent was treated as a mental illness requiring sentences in psychiatric institutions.

In cases of widespread violence that exploded into genocide, all three values—equality, freedom, and peace—were the issues. Genocide has been the bane, shame, outrage, and bleakest symbol of the twentieth century. When Pope Francis visited Armenia in June 2016, he noted that the Armenian genocide (1915–1917) was "made possible by twisted racial, ideological, or religious aims . . . even to the point of planning the annihilation of entire peoples."[10] From 1966 to 1979 there were no fewer than three genocides that darkened global history: West Pakistan's murderous massacre in East Pakistan, the ethnic genocide in Burundi and Rwanda, and the ideological genocide in Cambodia.

The first occurred in former East Pakistan (now Bangladesh) at the hands of the West Pakistani army. The relationship between East and West Pakistan had long been tense. First came the issue of political and military power in relation to size of population. In 1971, East Pakistan had a larger population (75 million, or 58 percent of the total), but West Pakistan wielded the political and military power; from 1950 to 1970, it took 60 percent of the budget. In culture, there was tension over choosing a common language for a modern nation (Urdu in the West and Bengali in the East), and there were religious differences: 97 percent of the West was Muslim, 15 percent of the East was Hindu. In November 1970, the Bhola Cyclone, the deadliest tropical cyclone on record, killed from three hundred thousand to five hundred thousand in East Pakistan. In its aftermath, West Pakistan dragged its feet in providing relief aid; a situation that heightened the bitter anger between the two. In national elections in late 1970, the Awami League, the largest party in East Pakistan, won a landslide victory; but West Pakistani officials refused to let Sheikh Mujibur Rahman, the leader of the league, become prime minister. Rahman, forcefully reacting, declared independence from West Pakistan and the birth of Bangladesh.

The day before, West Pakistan had launched Operation Searchlight, a massive military campaign to systematically "eliminate" Bengali students and intelligentsia, religious minorities, armed personnel, and as many civilians as possible; they especially targeted Hindus. This was at a time when the Nixon administration was using the Pakistani president, Yahya Khan, as the main link to China when National Security Advisor Henry Kissinger was preparing Nixon's visit to Beijing. Continuing to wear their Cold War lenses that saw rampant communism everywhere, Nixon and Kissinger refused to recognize that Rahman had rightfully won a landslide election and refused to believe or even respond to the accurate and courageous reports of Archer Blood, the US counsel general in Dacca, that the West Pakistan army was engaged in a bloody genocide in East Pakistan. Kissinger called Blood "this maniac." Washington refused to cut arms sales to West Pakistan and continued to ignore the ongoing genocide. The US would do nothing to jeopardize its tie to Yahya Khan, the launcher—with US connivance—of the genocide but an ally in the war on communism. India, however, which remained neutral in the Cold War, was, from Washington's perspective, a country to be mocked and scorned. Nixon told Kissinger that the Indians needed "a mass famine." When push came to shove, power politics had little time for humanitarian concerns or human rights.[11]

West Pakistan's military forces engaged in mass murder, rape, and deportation. The estimate of Bengalis killed ranged from three hundred thousand to three million; the number raped was estimated to be two to three hundred thousand. Some Islamic clerics issued fatwas (orders) urging soldiers to rape more Bengali women, especially Hindus, as they saw the conflict as a holy war. Ten million from Bangladesh fled to India, and thirty million were internally displaced. In the end, through the horror, Bangladesh had come into being in 1971, no longer a part of Pakistan.

In East Africa, the ethnic tribal division between the Hutus and the Tutsis led to another genocide. Though both resided primarily in Burundi and Rwanda, they also maintained a significant population in Uganda, Tanzania, and Zaire (renamed the Democratic Republic of Congo in 1997). In short, the whole region continually dealt with this ethnic problem. In the 1960s and 1970s, Hutus made up 86 percent

On an early, fog-encased morning in 1971, a rifle-bearing Bengali mother emerges from hiding her children from the enemy to get them food. (The roles of the men on the left of the rice field are unclear. Given recent history of the genocide, tempers were frayed. The men on the edges could have been charged with surveillance of this Bengali woman and her children or could be just standing watching what the family was doing.) Penny Tweedie/Alamy Stock Photo A1F4B7

of the population of Burundi with the Tutsis numbering 13 percent. However, the Belgian colonizers had favored the Tutsis until independence in 1962. Afterward, the Tutsis maintained control of almost all senior government and military posts. Throughout the 1960s, at least 100,000 Hutus and Tutsis were massacred in intertribal warfare. In April 1972, the majority Hutus rebelled against the controlling Tutsis. The Tutsis responded with killings en masse: between 80,000 and 210,000 Hutus were cut down. Several hundred thousand Hutus fled to Rwanda, Zaire, and Tanzania. The 1972 genocide left a permanent mark on the collective memory of the Hutus. In the years after, until the early 1990s, tensions continued to escalate between Burundi and Rwanda, with cross-border violence and large-scale killings by both sides.

A prelude to the Cambodian genocide was the war between the United States and Vietnam (1955–1973). Tape recordings of telephone messages between top American policymakers shockingly underscore the reality that they did not understand the war in Vietnam; they saw it as blatant communist aggression instead of a war for national independence. South Vietnamese lawyer and banker Truong Nhu Tang, who helped establish the National Liberation Front (NLF) that fought the South Vietnamese government and the United States, evaluated the US position: American leaders "suffered from an inability to enter into the mental world of their enemy and so to formulate policies that would effectively frustrate the strategies arrayed against them."[12] They also did not know how to extricate themselves from the war. So, they simply (and to no avail) continued to up the ante by sending more and more troops, the first of several tens of thousands in 1965; by early 1969, troop numbers had soared to over 540,000. A destructive air war over North Vietnam was ineffective in defeating the North or even slowing its shipments and troops down the Ho Chi Minh Trail into the South. Despite American claims of seeing "the light at the end of the tunnel," the Tet Offensive of the North Vietnamese army and the southern-based NLF in early 1968 shocked Americans that such a widespread attack—which reached the American embassy in Saigon—could come at that point in the war. The US government began a policy of "Vietnamization"—turning the war over to the Army of the Republic of Vietnam and allowing American troops to be withdrawn.

President Nixon began bombing Cambodian border areas often used by northern troops and the NLF as safe havens, in many cases pushing them farther into Cambodia. The United States did not notify or get the approval of the Cambodian government for the bombing campaign (which lasted from 1969 to 1973). In April 1970, under the pretexts of protecting remaining servicemen in the South and claiming to have discovered the "command center" directing the war, Nixon invaded Cambodia, thereby extending the war deep into that country. Pockets of Cambodian communist guerrillas (the Khmer Rouge) began to appear in the countryside. The US war in Vietnam ended in 1973 with a peace agreement with the North, while the war between the North and South ended in 1975 with a North Vietnamese victory. The war in Cambodia also ended in 1975 with the fall of the capital to the Khmer Rouge, who from 1975 to 1979 set in motion a tragic plan based on agrarian socialism in the mode of Mao and Stalin. The goal ultimately was to rid Cambodia of anyone connected to the old way of life, especially elements of bourgeois Westernization. Mass executions, torture, forced labor and relocation, disease, and malnutrition resulted in the estimated deaths of 25 percent of the population, about two million. One scholar has commented that this genocide was "an experiment in

Half-dressed, youthful troops of the US Ninth Infantry fight in the Tet Offensive.
They are firing on enemy troops (North Vietnamese and the southern-based
National Liberation Front) somewhere along the border. They are fighting on their
own initiative without direct orders from officers, an indication of the guerrilla
nature of the war at that time. Photo by Larry Burrows/Time Magazine/The LIFE
Picture Collection via Getty Images

social mobilization unmatched in twentieth-century revolutions."[13] The
genocide was ended ironically by war when Vietnam invaded Cambodia.

In China, in the wake of the disasters of the Great Leap Forward
and the Great Famine, came another catastrophe: an ideological and
political campaign that skirted on insanity. Mao had lost considerable
power in the Great Leap, and he schemed to retrieve it through the
Great Proletarian Cultural Revolution (1966–1976). The goal was to
use young people in paramilitary Red Guard units to destroy everything traditional or Western. In building a personality cult as a godlike
"Red Sun," Mao called his Red Guard minions to wage perpetual revolution against "revisionists" and "capitalist roaders" who sought to
undo the revolution (actually, to challenge Mao). "Struggle sessions"
against designated feudal "Black" figures, waged by properly "Red"
Guards, included verbal and physical abuse, torture, humiliation, imprisonment, or seizure of private property, and often ended in murder
or suicide. Historical sites and artifacts, especially religious ones, were
destroyed. An estimated 36 million people were persecuted and 750,000

to 1.5 million were killed, with as many permanently injured. In the end, to halt the insanity he had set loose, Mao forcibly sent millions of former Red Guards (some for many years) to far peripheral areas in the north and northwest "to learn from the peasantry." The military struggles were generally over by 1969, but the fratricidal factionalism continued until Mao's death in 1976.

Playing a role in and altering China's national and global viewpoints was its relationship with the USSR, which in the first decade of the People's Republic of China had been Beijing's strongest supporter and advisor in efforts to build up its heavy industry. But Mao's Great Leap flew in the face of Soviet advice, and Moscow resented Mao's increasingly bold assertions about China now being the proper leader of the world communist bloc. Acrimony mushroomed into antagonism. In 1960, the Soviets stormed out of China, withdrawing all advisors, taking blueprints of planned industrial projects, and cutting off all aid. By 1969 there were armed clashes between Chinese and the Soviet troops along river borders between Manchuria and Siberia. Given the estrangement between the two communist giants, China was open to changes in its relationship with the United States, which was also looking for some sort of rapprochement with the country. Nixon's surprising visit to Beijing in February 1972 culminated with the Shanghai Communique, which set the general framework for the new relationship: recognition by both sides of "one-China." The year 1979 brought the establishment of full diplomatic relations between the two long-time enemies.

Despite the United States' and USSR's continuing use of new African nations as proxies in the Cold War (particularly Angola and Mozambique), the 1970s saw an easing of tensions between the two superpowers. The United States became the Soviet Union's principal supplier of grain from 1975 to 1980. In space, the July 1975 Apollo-Soyuz Test Project was a sign of thawed relations: manned Apollo and Soyuz spacecraft docked in orbit, the first such link-up of the two nations in space. The two nations agreed to the Strategic Arms Limitation Talks (SALT) and in 1972 signed the Anti-Ballistic Missile (ABM) Treaty (which limited the anti-ballistic missile systems defending against ABM-delivered nuclear weapons). SALT 2 talks began in late 1972, and a treaty was negotiated but never ratified by the US Senate. In addition, the two powers signed with others such landmark treaties as the Outer Space Treaty (1967), which established international space law; the Nuclear Non-Proliferation Treaty (1970)—extended indefinitely in 1995—which dealt with nonproliferation, disarmament, and the right to use peaceful nuclear technology; the Seabed Treaty (1971), which outlawed nuclear weapons on the ocean floor; and the Biological Weapons Treaty (1972), which banned biological warfare.

The Soviet Union had troubles in its East European domains: among them, the 1950s crisis in Hungary and Polish riots in 1970, protesting higher food prices. The largest rebellion came in Czechoslovakia—"Prague Spring" that lasted from January through August 1968. The key figure was Alexander Dubcek (1921–1992), the first secretary of the Communist Party of Czechoslovakia. Son of a Slovakian cabinet-maker and Communist Party member, Dubcek was educated in Kyrgyzstan, where his family lived from 1925 to 1938. He joined the anti-German resistance in World War II and the Communist Party and worked his way up the ranks. His reform-minded goal in 1968—to provide "socialism with a human face"—focused on allowing substantial freedom of expression, tolerating organizations that were not under communist control, and decentralizing administrative control, the last most upsetting to the Soviets. Perceiving Dubcek as a high threat, the Soviet Union in late August 1968 sent two hundred thousand Warsaw Pact troops and five thousand tanks into Czechoslovakia. There was no military resistance. In the months that followed, the Czechs chose the strategy of nonviolent resistance: defiance of curfews, attempted fraternization with the enemy, and disrupting military activity by painting over and turning street signs to confuse the invaders and slow their progress. Dubcek accurately predicted the future that would become reality in two decades, "You can crush the flowers, but you can't stop the spring." In the aftermath of the Warsaw Pact invasion, Prague Spring's achievements died gradually. Dubcek was forced to resign in April 1969 and was expelled from the Party in 1970. His reputation as an enlightened, progressive socialist continued well after his 1992 death in a suspicious auto accident.

In 1973, the Arab members of OPEC (Organization of the Petroleum Exporting Countries) chose to use oil as a weapon in the Yom Kippur War in which Egypt and Syria invaded Israel to try to win back territory (the Sinai Peninsula and the Golan Heights, respectively) that they had lost in the Six-Day War (1967). They raised the price of oil, ultimately from three dollars to twelve dollars a barrel; they also initiated substantial cutbacks in production. Finally, they placed an embargo against the United States, the United Kingdom, Canada, Japan, and the Netherlands. The world financial system was already under pressure from the unilateral decision of the United States in 1971 to abandon the gold standard, under which the value of the currency was defined in terms of gold for which the currency could be exchanged; this action ended the 1944 Bretton Woods system. In the resulting floating exchange rate system, no official currency value was maintained. Other countries' currencies were pegged (tied) to the dollar, leaving their values to float.

The economic recession of the 1970s began with the huge surge in oil prices; in the United States price controls on gasoline meant long lines at gasoline pumps for consumers. In Western Europe there were also long lines and often-empty petrol pumps. The embargo, price hikes, and economic ripple effects were not uniform. The Europeans imported roughly 80 percent of their oil from the Middle East, and the Japanese over 90 percent. The United States, in contrast, imported only 12 percent of their oil from that region. Apart from a general global recession in the decade, inflation and unemployment remained high while economic growth slowed—a situation called "stagflation." In addition to the economic impact of the oil "shock," the episode brought on several interrelated realizations: oil reserves were finite, alternative energy sources had to be tapped (nuclear, sun, and wind), energy conservation prioritized, and the search for more oil reserves expedited. The sobering facts were that unless more reserves of oil, gas, and coal were found, oil would be gone by 2052, gas by 2060, and coal by 2088. The oil crisis led naturally to greater environmental and ecological awareness and worry.

In the midst of the concern about the earth and its resources, the Green Revolution—successful initiatives to increase agricultural production especially in the developing world—flourished. Norman Borlaug (1914–2009), the "father of the Green Revolution" and winner of the 1970 Nobel Peace Prize, grew up on an Iowa farm. With a degree in forestry, he became a plant geneticist and pathologist, spearheading projects in Mexico, the Philippines, India, and Brazil. There he introduced high-yielding, disease-resistant varieties of cereal grains and worked to transplant modern management techniques to the developing world—building irrigation infrastructure; relying on machines; and providing pesticides, herbicides, and synthetic fertilizers. While criticisms about the consequences and implications of the Green Revolution have been raised, there is no doubt that it created a positive new world for many. From 1961 to 1985 cereal production in developing nations more than doubled. In India alone, the total wheat production soared from 7 million tons in 1968 to 76 million tons in 2000. For Borlaug, it was more than simply a matter of food. As he said in his Nobel speech in 1970, "Almost certainly . . . the first essential component of social justice is adequate food for all mankind. Food is the moral right of all who are born into this world. Yet today 50 percent of the world's population grows hungry."

While the Green Revolution showed the positive potential of human manipulation of the environment, there were three environmental disasters that occurred mostly from human complicity or error. The first involved a chemical factory on Minamata Bay on the west coast of Kyushu, the southernmost Japanese island. The factory had released methyl mercury in industrial wastewater into the bay since 1932; the mercury levels exceeded safety standards by four hundred times. The highly toxic chemical accumulated in fish and shellfish, which, when eaten, caused mercury poisoning. Altogether 10,000 people were poisoned to some degree; serious victims numbered 2,265, of which 1,784 died. Symptoms included muscle deterioration, numbness in hands and feet, damage to hearing and speech, paralysis, and death. Even after the disease became known in 1956, the chemical company incredibly enough continued to release the contaminated water into the bay until 1968. People were still dying of Minamata disease in the late 1980s.

The collapse of the Banqiao Dam in the Chinese province of Henan in August 1975 was the most destructive technical disaster ever. Rain deluges from the remnants of a typhoon poured forty inches of rain the first day of the flood with frequent downpours on succeeding days. The problem was the shoddy construction of the dam: cracks had begun to appear soon after its construction in 1952; the Soviets reinforced the structure using "Soviet specifications," dubbing it the "Iron Bridge" for its supposed invincibility. When the dam collapsed in the middle of the night, a tidal wave thirty-three feet high and seven miles wide in some places tore down the valley at speeds of fifty kilometers per hour. There was no early warning system or evacuation plans. At least 171,000 people lost their lives, and 11 million lost their homes.

In March 1979 in the United States, the Three-Mile Island nuclear power plant ten miles from Harrisburg, Pennsylvania, had a partial nuclear meltdown. After a pressure valve in a reactor failed to close, radiation-contaminated cool water drained from the open valve into adjoining buildings and the core began to dangerously overheat. The failure was both mechanical and human. No one was injured, and the large amount of radiated water that escaped and the radioactive gases released caused no measurable problem. Though the situation was handled in time, the unnerving fact was that the reactor was less than half an hour away from a complete meltdown.

In medicine, the 1970s produced technology with the potential not only to help diagnose a disease but also to indicate what stage the disease was in. The computed tomography scan (CT or CAT scan) became available in 1971; the first successful positron emission tomography

(PET scan) occurred in 1975; and magnetic resonance imaging (MRI) was invented in 1977. Vaccines for rubella and mumps were produced in 1966. In cardiac treatment, Dr. Christiaan Barnard in South Africa conducted the world's first human heart transplant in 1967; two years later came the first artificial heart implant. In 1973 the first genetically engineered organism was developed, a procedure by which new genes were inserted into other genetic material for various desired results. For example, in developing countries where vitamin intake was often inadequate, a gene taken from the carrot genome could be spliced into the genome of rice, so that the rice would also contain Vitamin B. Then, in a life-changing development, the world's first "test-tube" baby was born in 1978 through a process called in vitro fertilization, offering hope to childless couples.

In the realm of humanitarian medical activity among the poor and the sick, perhaps no one is more prominent in the twentieth century than Mother Teresa. Born Agnes Bojaxhiu in Skopje, Macedonia (1910), of Albanian heritage, she decided at age eighteen to become a nun. She went to Dublin, Ireland, to join the Sisters of Loreto. That order sent her to Darjeeling, India, for her novitiate, and there she taught at a high school for girls who came from the poorest Bengali families. In these years she learned to speak Bengali and Hindi fluently. She made her final profession of vows in 1937, at which time she became "Mother Teresa." In 1946, she recounted that she had received a "call within a call," that is, to work in Kolkata's slums to help the city's poorest and sickest. After six months of fundamental medical training, she set up a home for the dying and an open-air school. In 1950 she won recognition for her new congregation, the Missionaries of Charity, which, in the 1950s and 1960s, established an orphanage, nursing home, leper colony, a family clinic, and a number of mobile health clinics. By the 1960s, she had begun to receive acclaim from the Church and others for her work. She spoke before the UN General Assembly in 1985. She announced her Gift of Love on Christmas Eve of that year: setting up homes for men, women, and children with HIV/AIDS—the first a home for men in Greenwich Village. Others were established around the world; most famous was an orphanage in Addis Ababa, Ethiopia, for three hundred children with HIV/AIDS.

She received the Nobel Prize for Peace in 1979. The citation noted that her prize came "for work undertaken in the struggle to overcome poverty and distress, which also constitutes a threat to world peace" and that "a feature of her work has been respect for the individual human being, for his or her dignity and innate value." She was criticized by some for hewing to the Catholic position against contraception and abortion. At the time of her death, there were over four thousand Missionaries of Charity (in addition to thousands who volunteered) with 610 foundations in 123 countries around the globe. She epitomized the name she was called: the greatest humanitarian of the twentieth century. She was beatified by Pope John Paul II in 2003 and canonized as "St. Teresa of Calcutta" by Pope Francis on September 4, 2016.

CHAPTER 6

Bright Triumphs, Dark Disasters, 1980–1991

The earliest evidence of smallpox as a killer was found on the mummy of an Egyptian king who died in 1157 B.C.E. In the eighteenth century, the disease killed an estimated four hundred thousand people a year and caused one-third of all cases of blindness. In the twentieth century, the estimated number of people who died of smallpox was about three hundred million. Thus, the 1980 World Health Organization's announcement of its global eradication was an immensely bright medical beacon.

There were two other pandemics in the twentieth century. One was the Spanish flu in 1918, which infected a third of the world's population (five hundred million people) and killed up to one hundred million. The other—HIV/AIDS—began spreading in the United States in the 1970s, its source unknown until the 1980s. The thinking of the medical world was that HIV likely originated in the Democratic Republic of Congo about 1920 when the virus crossed species from chimpanzees to humans. It became a pandemic in the 1980s and beyond, infecting 78 million people around the globe and killing 40 million. The number of new HIV (human immunodeficiency virus) infections in 1990 was about 2 million; the numbers rose steadily to a high point of 3.5 million in 1997 and then stabilized around 2.5 million in the early twenty-first century. Deaths from AIDS (acquired immune deficiency syndrome) reached their pinnacle in the first decade of the twenty-first century. Yet the horror of the situation remained: until the mid-2010s about 5,000 people a day were infected with HIV. The pandemic raged most severely in sub-Saharan Africa, where 67 percent of all new HIV infections were found.

In contrast to the bleakness of HIV/AIDS, the world of technology beamed with two bright stars in these years: continued advances in space and in personal computers. In space, one focus was sending into orbit

The Twentieth Century: A World History. Keith Schoppa, Oxford University Press. © Oxford University Press 2021.
DOI: 10.1093/oso/9780190497354.003.0007

space stations manned by crews for extended periods of time to serve as labs for scientific research. The USSR's *Salyut* (fireworks) program produced the world's first crewed space station (1971–1986), followed by the first US space station, Skylab (1973–1979). The successes of the Salyut program (records set in mission duration, spacewalks, and the first orbital handover from one crew to another) gave rise to a multi-modular space station, Mir, "peace." Mir (1986–2001) was made up of seven pressurized modules, each launched into orbit separately over ten years and each designed to perform particular experiments or functions.

The Mir space station floats above planet Earth during the final shuttle-Mir fly around in 2001. Operated by the Soviet Union and later by Russia, it was the first modular space station, assembled in orbit from 1986 to 1996. It was at core a module where the astronauts lived and six docking ports that were used for re-supply vehicles and to lock on the specialized modules used for various technical work. NASA

Between 1981, when the United States began its space shuttle program, and 2011, the shuttle was the manned launch vehicle. Composed of an orbiter launched by two reusable rocket boosters and with a disposable external fuel tank, each vehicle had an operational life span of ten years and could theoretically be launched one hundred times. The shuttles serviced Mir, brought cosmonauts to the space station, brought American astronauts to work with the cosmonauts, and transported payloads of up to fifty thousand pounds. When a mission was completed, the orbiter could re-enter the atmosphere and land like a glider. Five shuttles (*Atlantis*, *Challenger*, *Columbia*, *Discovery*, and *Endeavor*) made 135 flights (many under ten days), but the program suffered two major disasters: the inflight explosions of *Challenger* (1986) and *Columbia* (2003), resulting in the deaths of their crews. During these years an unwritten, and perhaps even unspoken, agreement between the United States and USSR set spheres of sorts for each nation to explore the solar system: for the USSR, Venus, and for the United States, Mars and planets farther from the sun, including the outer limits of the solar system.

This exploration of interplanetary space provided much scientific information. The first successful interplanetary spacecraft, Mariner 2, was launched by the United States in August 1962 to fly by Venus and provide measurements of temperature and the magnetic field. Longer term exploration was achieved by Voyager 1 and 2 (launched in August and September 1977), Pioneer 10 (launched in March 1972), and Cassini-Huygens, an international project (in 1997). The Voyager explorations were expected to function until around 2020; they studied Jupiter, Uranus, Saturn, and Neptune, their moons and rings, and solar wind. In the second decade of the twenty-first century, Voyager 1 was at the very fringe of the solar system, more than nine billion miles from Earth; if it continued, it would become the first human-made object to enter interstellar space. Pioneer 10 reached Jupiter and provided close-up images and data. Cassini-Huygens explored Saturn and its largest moon, Titan. In 2004 when it reached Saturn, it began orbiting the planet; its detachable probe landed on Titan in 2005, recording data in a surface study. The Hubble Space Telescope, launched in 1990 to orbit 353 miles above Earth, provided pictures of unprecedented completeness and clarity of the furthest galaxies ever seen and of planets orbiting other stars. In addition, the International Space Station, launched in late 1998 and orbiting 248 miles above Earth, became a permanently occupied outer space outpost serving as a laboratory for new technologies and as an observation deck for research on astronomy and the Earth's geology and environment.

While new technology helped explore the vast solar system and beyond, the 1970s saw advances in the micro-scale world of the personal computer. The Information or Digital Age began about 1975, based on a technological leap from mechanical analog electronic technology to digital electronics—with the consequent proliferation of digital computers and record keeping. It represented a historic shift from traditional manufacturing industry to a culture based on the computerization of information that became, in effect, a commodity. A time when huge troves of information were collected and transmitted almost instantaneously, the Digital Age was a socioeconomic and intellectual revolution in which access to and control of information became the goal.

The vehicle for entering the Digital Age was the internet, the massive network of globally interlinked computer networks through which information could be exchanged. The internet was the "networking infrastructure." In the 1980s, Tim Berners-Lee invented the central information-sharing model, the World Wide Web (WWW), which he built on top of the internet. Berners-Lee, a British computer scientist, graduated from Oxford University with a physics degree, and he then worked at the largest particle physics lab in the world, CERN in Geneva, Switzerland. The WWW revolutionized the use of the computer; in 1990 for *Time* magazine, he wrote the first browser computer program.

In 1999, *Time* named him one of the hundred most important people of the twentieth century: "He wove the WWW, [creating] a mass medium for the twenty-first century. . . . And he more than anyone else has fought to keep it open, nonproprietary, and free."[1] He made the WWW publicly available, claiming no patent or royalties for himself. The number of internet users increased rapidly in the early twenty-first century: in 2005, there were about 940 million personal computers in the world; in 2015, there were over 2.8 billion. While some had predicted that the market for PCs had reached its peak, in 2020 the PC market had its first big growth in ten years. While home working and remote learning were the big drivers, people also turned to PCs and laptops for entertainment. Market research firm Canalys reported that PC shipments reached 297 million units in 2020, up an impressive 11 percent from 2019. IDC (IDC Corporate USA) puts the year's sales at 302 million shipments, up 13.1 percent year over year. Gartner, the third-largest vendor followed suit with Canalys and IDC, agreeing that 2020 was a big year for PCs and the biggest growth since 2010.[2]

For all the considerable bright beacons of the period, darkness in the form of disasters and calamities cast a pall. The worst industrial disaster in history occurred in Bhopal, India, on the night of December 2–3, 1984. A pesticide factory built by the American-based multinational Union Carbide Corporation (UCC) in the 1970s suspended operation in the early 1980s because of poor sales. The facilities were not maintained: the unit containing the deadly chemical methyl isocyanate (MIC)—five times more lethal than the World Wars I and II chemical weapon phosgene—needed refrigeration to prevent chemical reactions. However, electricity and refrigeration were cut off three months before the accident. Temperature and pressure gauges were not working; there was no alarm system. When the gas leak occurred, it created a dense poisonous cloud over the city of Bhopal, exposing five hundred thousand people who woke in coughing fits, their lungs filling with fluid. Autopsies of victims showed a gross increase in the weight of lungs of up to three times the normal. Estimates of those killed instantly and those who died from gas-related illnesses afterward totaled over twenty-five thousand. In 1989, UCC compensated claims of Bhopal victims in the amount of $470 million, about 15 percent of what India had requested. In addition, a spokesman from Bhopal told the BBC in 2014 that some 93 percent of victims were not compensated.[3] A three-year investigation by India's Interpol unit charged UCC with criminally negligent homicide. UCC arrogantly dismissed every summons and arrest warrant it received, arguing that, as a US corporation, it did not accept India's jurisdiction over it, a position that defied the basic tenets of international criminal law. In 2001, Dow Chemical Company purchased the UCC property, but it refused to pay anything more to Bhopal, arguing that everything relating to the gas tragedy had been settled.

Even more calamitous than Bhopal—for both the short and long term—was the explosion of a nuclear reactor at the Chernobyl nuclear plant near Pripyat, Ukraine. The causes: a design-flawed nuclear reactor operated by an inexperienced and inadequately trained staff. A chemical explosion, it catapulted an estimated ten tons of radioactive fuel and debris into the atmosphere—four hundred times more radioactive material than the Hiroshima bombing. Radioactive fallout was concentrated in Belarus, Ukraine, and Russia, though there were lesser levels of contamination over most of Europe. At least three hundred fifty thousand people from the Chernobyl area were forcibly resettled, ordered to leave their homes and almost all their belongings (for three days it was said); in the end, they were never allowed to return.

Pripyat was the base city of the Chernobyl Nuclear Power Plant, sixty-five miles northwest of the city of Kiev. Built starting in 1970, it was to be the home of the authorities and workers at the plant. The explosion came at 1:23 a.m. on April 26, 1986. Evacuation of Pripyat began at 2:00 p.m. on April 27, roughly thirty-six hours after the explosion: forty-three thousand residents evacuated on twelve hundred buses brought in from Kiev, which was completed in three and a half hours. It was all a matter of miraculous timing and space—where a person was at the time of the explosion's impact, when the plant fire was raging out of control, or when the change in wind direction or wind velocity might alter the volume of radiation carried by the wind. It was completely a matter of chance: individual life would go on, but certainly not as imagined, not as planned.

The post-explosion experiences of none of the residents of Pripyat can have been good, what with the news of men at the plant dying almost immediately from radiation poisoning, with concerns about the levels of radiation in the city, and with worried questions about the evacuation of all residents. One resident compels our attention for revealing clearly the human costs of the accident: twenty-three-year-old Lyudmilla Ignatenko was married to twenty-five-year-old Vasily Ignatenko, a fireman. He was one of the first responders after the explosion, suffered a lethal dosage of radiation, and died two weeks later. Lyudmilla was carrying their first child when he died.

> We had been married for three years. We lived in the dormitory of the fire station [in Pripyat] where he worked. We and three other couples shared a kitchen. The red fire-trucks were parked on the ground level. At about 1:30 a.m., I heard three trucks preparing to leave from the station. I called down to Vasily from our balcony to ask where they were going. "The nuclear power plant is on fire," he said. They weren't wearing their canvas gear. They went off just as they were, in their shirt sleeves. No one had told them [about the rapidity and ominous and horrors of radiation poisoning]. "Go to sleep. I'll wake you when I get home."
>
> I didn't see the explosion itself. Just the flames. Everything was radiant: the whole sky. A tall flame. And smoke. The heat was awful. And he's still not back. At seven in the morning, I was told he was in the hospital. He was all swollen and puffed up. You could barely see his eyes.
>
> On that very first day [when I returned to the dormitory from the hospital], they measured me with a dosimeter. My clothes, bag, purse, and shoes—they were all "hot." And they took that all away from me right there—even my underwear.

He started to change; every day I met a brand-new person. The burns started to come to the surface. In his mouth, on his tongue, on his cheeks at first there were little lesions, and then they grew. [His skin] came off in layers—as a white filmy substance. He became covered with boils. When he turned his head, there would be a clump of hair left on the pillow. I tried joking: "It's convenient, you don't need a comb."

When they all [the radiation-poisoned patients] died, they refurbished the hospital. They scraped down the walls and dug up the parquet. When he died, they dressed him up in formal wear, with his service cap. They couldn't get his shoes on, because his feet had swollen up. They buried him barefooted. My love! The only thing that saved me was it happened so fast; there wasn't any time to think; there wasn't any time to cry.[4]

The environmental impact was devastating. Land significantly contaminated with fallout totaled 38,610 square miles. Agricultural land removed for a period from cultivation totaled 1,938,100 acres, with 1,715,000 acres of forestland also set aside. An 18 square-mile area surrounding the nuclear plant and its contiguous town Pripyat was made an exclusion zone or no-man's land; it will not be safe to return for three thousand years—the year 4986. A long-term problem is a more than two-yard-wide, two-thousand-ton mass of metal, concrete, and uranium that pooled beneath the exploded reactor; as it cooled, it turned into a solid mass filled with radioactive material, now called the "Elephant's Foot" for its wrinkled appearance. Anyone who approached it in 1986 would have received a fatal dose of radiation in less than a minute. Even in 2017, being in the room with the mass for five minutes would mean one had only two days to live. The Elephant's Foot will remain radioactive for 100,000 years. In May 1986, workers began to build a sarcophagus, a giant concrete enclosure to seal off radiation from the inside. All those who worked on the sarcophagus were dead within a year or so. How and when to try to remove the Elephant's Foot without another emission of radioactivity remained a huge issue.[5]

Various medical models projected the number of those who would die of cancer. By 2006 there were an estimated thousand cases of thyroid cancer and four thousand deaths from other cancers; models show that by 2065 there would be, at minimum, sixteen thousand deaths from thyroid cancer and twenty-five thousand deaths from other cancers.[6]

Another ecological disaster struck in March 1989, when an oil tanker, the *Exxon Valdez*, struck Alaska's Bligh Reef in Prince William Sound. Eleven million gallons of crude oil (257,000 barrels) spilled into the ocean; its volume roughly equivalent to the amount of water necessary

The extent of the Chernobyl nuclear disaster is illustrated by this field near an abandoned building in Pripyat. It is filled with gas masks left behind in the general panic to escape. © Torsten Pursche/Shutterstock 547730746

to fill seventeen Olympic-size swimming pools. One of the most devastating human-caused environmental disasters in history, the crude oil spill covered 1,300 miles of coastline and 11,000 square miles of ocean. The spill had catastrophic impacts on the area's wildlife: the best estimates are that about 250,000 seabirds, 2,800 sea otters, 300 harbor seals, 250 bald eagles, up to 22 killer whales, and billions of salmon and herring were killed.[7] Apart from these major crises, attention turned in the 1970s and after to the impacts of economic development on the environment, especially the problems of acid rain, the greenhouse effect, air and marine pollution, land degradation, deforestation, desertification, and species extinction. In December 1983, the UN secretary-general appointed former Norwegian prime minister Gro Harlem Brundtland to establish and chair the UN's World Commission for Environment and Development—what became known as the Brundtland Commission. The first Scandinavian woman to serve as prime minister, she was a physician by training. She served in Norway's government as minister of the environment from 1974 to 1979. A leader in the Norwegian Labor Party, she was the most influential politician during the 1980s and early 1990s. She earned a reputation for her success at being able to deal with difficult conflicts through her logical and problem-solving mind, her charisma, and her amiability. Her approach to conflict resolution was nicknamed the "Gro grip." Often in Norwegian media releases, Brundtland was referred to as "mother earth" or "mother of the nation." The Brundtland Commission studied crucial environmental issues and suggested possible solutions. Its final report, *Our Common Future*, called for strategies for "sustainable development," defined as "development that meets the needs of the present without compromising the ability of future generations to meet their own needs."[8]

One historical case study in the report pointing to the difficulty of sustainable development concerned the Amazon rainforest. In the late 1980s, western Brazil ranchers were burning the rainforest to clear areas for ranches and for modern roads, contributing, scientists said, to global warming. Rubber tappers whose livelihood depended on rainforest rubber trees opposed the ranchers. At one point, 130 ranchers in the state of Acre expelled about 100,000 tappers from the forest. The tappers' leader, Chico Mendes, one of seventeen siblings, was the son of a poor tapper. He had no formal education, learning to read only at age eighteen. Mendes helped organize and served as president of his village's rural workers union, which resisted deforestation, often confronting men on bulldozers with chainsaws in hand. In 1985, Mendes founded the National Council of Rubber Tappers, working to establish rain forest reserves. He described his goals: "At first I thought I was fighting to save rubber trees; then I thought I was trying to save the Amazon rainforest; now I realize I am fighting for humanity." The UN Environmental Program granted him the 1987 Global 500 Award "for environmental activism in the face of immense social, political, and logistical obstacles." Then, on a 1988 December night, he was shot to death outside his home by a local rancher, enraged by his environmental agenda. His tragic death could not overshadow his legacy: he was a local activist whose environmental involvement transcended the local, making a lasting mark on our world.

Two especially futile wars and a temporarily conclusive one also marked the decade. The Iran-Iraq War (1980–1988) began ostensibly as a territorial dispute over the Shatt al-Arab River, which formed the boundary between the two nations; most of the large battles in this eight-year war were fought in the river's vicinity. Although Iraq's Saddam Hussein invaded Iran in September 1980, the course of the war fit a pattern: Iraq was forced into a continual defensive mode as it faced repeated Iranian offensives. Despite the number of casualties—at least half a million—and billions of dollars' worth of damages, neither side saw any real gains from the brutal war that featured indiscriminate ballistic-missile attacks and the extensive use of chemical weapons, On March 16, 1988, Iraq carried out history's largest chemical weapons attack directed against a civilian-populated area—the Kurdish town of Halabja (population 40,000) in northern Iraq; it had just fallen to the Iranian army and Kurdish guerrillas. Bombs of chemical agents— especially mustard gas and the deadly nerve agent sarin—were dropped; they killed 3,200 to 5,000 (mostly civilians) and injured 7,000 to 10,000. The Iraq High Criminal Court in 2010 acknowledged that the Halabja massacre was an act of genocide.

Unknown at the time was US complicity regarding the Iraqi use of chemical weapons. During the war, the United States wholeheartedly supported Saddam Hussein and the Iraqi cause and was aware that Iraq was using poison gas. Central Intelligence Agency (CIA) documents show specifically that senior US officials since the early 1980s were regularly briefed on the scale and nature of Iraq's chemical attacks.[9] In early 1988 before the Halabja attack, the Iraqis had used mustard gas and sarin in four other offensives in which they relied on US satellite imagery, maps, and other intelligence freely supplied by the US government. The apparent attitude of the Reagan administration was that it was better to let the attacks continue if they could lead to an Iraqi victory. In March 1988, the United States learned from satellite imagery that Iran was soon likely to gain a significant strategic advantage that might lead to military victory by capitalizing on a major hole in Iraqi defensive positions. President Reagan sent a note to Secretary of Defense Frank Carlucci: "An Iranian victory is unacceptable."[10] So, US intelligence supplied the usual information to Iraq—satellite imagery and maps—about Iranian positions and movements, Iranian logistics facilities, and air defense. The result was Halabja and more gas attacks to follow on the Fao (al-Faw) Peninsula, southeast of the Iraqi city of Basra. The United States did not mention Halabja much again until 2003, when George W. Bush used it as one of the reasons for the US invasion of Iraq in that year—an irony since the United States made Halabja possible.

The temporarily conclusive war in this region was fought in early 1991. In August 1990, Iraq, still under Saddam Hussein, invaded Kuwait, angry over Kuwaiti oil policy; in less than a week, Iraq announced its formal annexation. In November, the UN Security Council authorized military intervention in Iraq if it did not withdraw its forces by January 15, 1991. The Gulf War broke out on January 16 with air strikes; the United States, joined by thirty-eight nations, sent ground forces in early

February. Iraqi troops and Saddam Hussein began to retreat to Baghdad on February 26. In the end, Kuwait was freed but critical Iraqi issues remained.

The second futile war in this period was the USSR in Afghanistan. On December 24, 1979, the USSR undertook its first military operation outside the Eastern bloc since World War II—to support the communist government in Afghanistan, which was facing a growing insurgency. Taking Kabul in a storm of military might (280 transport aircraft with three divisions of 25,500 men), the Soviets on December 27 engineered a coup: murdering the current president and installing in his stead a pro-Moscow faction leader. The new president undertook astonishingly progressive reforms, moving toward a constitution with basic democratic rights. Most controversially, he championed women's rights, especially compulsory education for girls and marriage reforms, including the prohibition of bride price—both of which threatened patriarchal structures and traditions.

Anahita Ratebzad, the face of feminism in Afghanistan from the 1950s to 1986, was the daughter of a provincial subgovernor who was arrested for supporting a reformist regime. Anahita, only a few years old at the time, never saw him again, but she was determined to follow his path of service and reform. From 1950 to 1954 she studied nursing at the University of Michigan; she graduated from Kabul University's Medical School in 1962. In the late 1950s and 1960s she was the country's foremost outspoken and controversial female activist. She was one of four women elected to the Parliament in 1965, and in the same year she co-founded the Communist Party, known as the People's Democratic Party of Afghanistan (PDPA). In May 1978, less than a month after the PDPA seized control of the country, the *New Kabul Times* quoted her: "Educating and enlightening women is now the subject of close government attention."[11] When the Soviets occupied the country (1979–1989), she served as a member of the Politburo and the Revolutionary Council and was founder and head of the Democratic Organization of Afghan Women. Because her speeches brought together feminist and head of state international themes, she served as a bridge from the Afghan communist regime to progressive regimes outside the Soviet bloc.[12]

Insurgency against the communist government and the Soviet invasion rose in fierce resistance. The reforms inspired rebellion, as did the very presence of Soviet forces, atheist or Christian, who were to many Afghans a blasphemy of Islam. Proclaiming a jihad (literally, "struggling"; often taken to mean a "holy war"), the mujahideen (those fighting a jihad) gained support throughout the Islamic world for their guerrilla units that controlled 80 percent of the country's territory. Steadily increasing monetary support came from the CIA, Pakistan, and Saudi Arabia; CIA support totaled $500,000 in 1979, $20 to $30 million in 1980, and $630 million in 1987. The United States gave 1,000 US-built shoulder-launched Stinger anti-aircraft missiles to the mujahideen in 1986–1987. Many experts contend that the Stingers helped turned the tide of war after 1987 because they allowed the mujahideen to easily shoot down Soviet planes and helicopters. Both the mujahideen and the Soviet army (numbering at any time from 80,000 to 104,000 soldiers) caused great destruction: about 15,000 Soviet soldiers were killed, about 2 million Afghans died in the war, and about 7 million fled as refugees, many to Pakistan and Iran.

With no victory in sight and the troops greatly demoralized, the Soviets under Mikhail Gorbachev pulled out, the last soldier leaving in February 1989. They had accomplished nothing. But the war had severe unintended consequences for the Soviets. They were faced with heavy financial losses in the war and from the Chernobyl calamity. The resulting financial instability was an important factor in the USSR's 1991 total collapse. Further, there were unintended consequences for US actions: funding the mujahedeen and putting Stinger missiles into their hands gave rise ultimately to a dark and bleak situation. After the Soviets left, some mujahedeen began to fight each other, giving rise to political and social chaos. To end the internecine fighting and supposedly bring stability, a new force, the Taliban emerged. Originally, this was a student group from Kandahar who had attended ultra-radical Islamic fundamentalist schools in Pakistan; they also had ties to the former Kandahar mujahideen. With their emphasis on sharia (Islamic law), they were both retrogressive in terms of the state of society and culture and aggressive indeed, taking over the whole country by 1996. After they seized power, they supported Osama bin Laden and his terrorist al-Qaeda network. In the end, inadvertently to be sure, US policy sowed the seeds for the rise of the Taliban and Islamic terrorism against the West.

Gorbachev, secretary-general of the USSR's Communist Party from 1985 to 1991, favored reform. Given the USSR's dire financial instability, especially in the aftermath of Chernobyl and the Afghan war, he began to talk about *perestroika* (economic restructuring). Coupled with that need and aware of his European satellite states' restiveness, he also championed *glasnost* (openness), specifically calling for leadership that operated in an open, consultative government with a broader communication of information.

Already in 1980, Poland had broached major reform, organizing the first independent trade union in the Soviet sphere, Solidarity, led by Lech Walesa. Although Poland's communist leader suspended the union and imprisoned its leaders, it remained an underground organization with growing political force and the support of the Catholic Church. For his nonviolent approach and unifying goals, Walesa won the Nobel Peace Prize in 1983. In 1988, through a series of national strikes, Solidarity forced the government to agree to have an open dialogue with the union. Both sides agreed to form a bicameral legislature (the National Assembly), with the upper house elected by the people. Walesa was elected to serve as Poland's president (1990–1995). It is significant that the Soviets did not invade Poland or take forcible steps to "keep" Poland "in line," unlike their violent reactions to earlier reform attempts in Hungary (1956) and Czechoslovakia (1968).

The other Warsaw Pact nations and the constituent Soviet Republics all had different patterns for cutting their ties to the USSR and moving to elections, multiparty parliamentary systems, and basic political rights. Hungary, like Poland, had enacted some reforms in the 1980s, whetting its appetite for more in its first election, in March 1990. East Germany, which had constructed the Berlin Wall in 1961 to keep East Germans from crossing the border, declared the wall opened in November 1989 (though it was not completely dismantled until 1992). The East German decision to open the wall came in the midst of a growing crisis. The contextual background: the rapid political changes in Eastern Europe where the old communist leadership was quickly losing power. It faced huge demonstrations (in Leipzig, up to three hundred thousand in number; in Berlin, up to half a million) of people demanding free elections and movement toward a free market system. As a mark of their out-of-touch attitudes and policies, the East German authorities issued the military shoot-to-kill orders and lobbied Moscow to send in the Soviet army under the Warsaw Pact to restore order and protect communism. By this time, however, Soviet leaders thought it impractical to continue to exercise control over the Eastern bloc.

East Germany held elections in March 1990, and West and East Germany were reunited in October 1990. The "Velvet Revolution" in Czechoslovakia was, as the name implies, nonviolent. Peaceful street demonstrations, numbering as many as eight hundred thousand protestors in Prague, and news of what was happening across Eastern Europe led the communist government to dismantle the one-party state. Writer and philosopher Vaclav Havel was heavily involved in the demonstrations. At the Prague rally pictured, the sign "Havel na Hrad," often held by demonstrators with Havel's photograph, means

This student rally on December 28, 1989, at Prague's Wenceslas Square celebrated the election of Vaclav Havel, author, dissident, and politician, to the presidency during the Velvet Revolution—November 17 to December 29, 1989, when the Communist government for Czechoslovokia was peacefully overthrown. Photo by Steve Eason/Hulton Archive/Getty Images 79158468

"Havel to the castle"—where the head of state resided. This rallying cry was an accurate prediction: Havel was elected the last president of Czechoslovakia in 1989. After that, the country split into Slovakia and the Czech Republic, and he served as first president of the Czech Republic (1993–2003).

Bulgaria shared the peaceful nature of the revolutions in Poland, Hungary, and Czechoslovakia. Romania was the only East European Soviet Republic that saw violence, not from the USSR, but internally. There, the party dictator, Nicolae Ceauşescu, decided to ride out the 1989 anticommunist storm, using the army to mow down 1,104 demonstrators. But then the army as a whole suddenly sided with the demonstrators; Ceauşescu and his wife tried to escape a military and civilian riot at party headquarters, but they were caught and summarily executed.

The fervent nationalism in Eastern Europe ignited similar nationalism among the Soviet Republics. The Baltic States came first, with Estonia declaring its independence in November 1988 and Lithuania

An immense crowd of 100,000 listened desultorily to Ceauşescu's last speech from the balcony of the Communist Party headquarters in Bucharest on December 25, 1989. Within minutes, they totally drowned out his voice with their mockeries, screams, taunts, jeers, and fireworks. The demise of Ceauşescu came astoundingly quickly; after a two-hour military trial, he and his wife were summarily executed on Christmas afternoon, 1989. Reuters/Radu Sigheti RP1DRILEAWAB and Latvia in March 1989. Moscow threatened military action and economic sanctions but did not intervene. Instead, local pro-Soviet special police units trained as paramilitary forces tried unsuccessfully to suppress the demonstrations in Latvia and Lithuania in early 1991.

A Moscow coup attempt of hard-liners against Gorbachev and his reforms failed in August 1991, but his power was irreversibly gutted; a few weeks later Moscow granted the Baltic States their independence. To cite a phrase Gorbachev had used about its European satellite states, that autumn the Soviet Union "crumble[d] like a dry saltine cracker," with its member Republics each declaring independence, some in the midst of violence, others peacefully. A crucial step came on December 1 when the second most powerful Republic, Ukraine, seceded. A week later Boris Yeltsin, who had emerged a key leader in the Russian Republic, met with the leaders of Ukraine and Belarus. Signed December 8, 1991, in a village in Belarus, the Belavezha Accord stated that the Soviet Union was dead; on December 21, 1991, in the Alma-Ata Protocol, signed in Kazakhstan, eleven other Republics affirmed the USSR's dissolution. Whereas glasnost had unraveled the seams of state, it was perestroika that plunged the world's most powerful socialist state into oblivion. As Gorbachev said in his farewell address before his resignation on Christmas Day: "The old [command economic] system fell apart even before the new system [the market economy] began to work."[13] The Soviet Union was no more. Whether these were signs of brightness or darkness depended on one's perspective. The Cold War was over.

The wave of liberalization that had swept over the communist world was also replicated in the People's Republic of China (PRC). Deng Xiaoping, the new Chinese leader after the death of Mao in 1976, undertook economic reforms in 1980—in actuality, a market economy but which the pragmatist Deng called, in a face-saving way, "socialism with Chinese characteristics." This was not an objective criterion; it simply stood for whatever policymakers said about how they practiced the economy. Economic liberalization, as it had in Eastern Europe and the Soviet Union, opened the door to the possibility of political change. In late 1986 students began to call for reforms. Communist Party Chairman Hu Yaobang, an avid political reformer, was scapegoated for their demonstrations and forced to resign. His death on April 15, 1989, set off seven weeks of escalating demonstrations at Tiananmen (the Gate of Heavenly Peace) Square in Beijing, where students, in the middle of a hunger strike, stridently called for democracy and the end of party-government corruption. Out of an exaggerated fear of anarchy and counterrevolution, Deng eventually had enough, sending the army on June 4 to clear the Square and end the protests. Amid talk and actions of killings and repression, Deng spun fantasies of political liberalization.

South Africa seemed to be in almost the same mode as the PRC, in the 1980s sinking ever-more deeply into a military police state. After the Sharpeville massacre of 1960, the state started expanding the army: universal conscription for one year of service was enacted in 1967. A decade later it was increased to two years, with thirty days service per year for the following eight years. The number of conscripts who did not report for duty began to escalate, and the number of conscientious objectors rose as well. P. W. Botha, a staunch apartheid hard-liner, became president in 1978, implementing his "total strategy" to build and consolidate a statewide security plan, basically turning the government into a military bureaucracy.

In 1981, the Botha administration enacted a law specifying that troops in the South Africa Defence Force (SADF) would be stationed in black townships and Bantustans as part of the territorial apartheid policy. The first occupying troops entered the townships in October 1984, leading to black rural uprisings and violent demonstrations that were met by harsh SADF repression. Botha declared two states of emergency under which martial law held sway: in July 1985 for thirty-six townships, and in June 1986 for the whole country. From 1985 to 1989, thousands of blacks were detained or killed. In 1988, whites made up 14.8 percent of the population; blacks, 74.1 percent. Whites had rights and freedom; blacks, in contrast, were isolated on black reservations, without rights, without freedom.

South Africa was increasingly isolated, treated as an international pariah. Most of the world boycotted South African products. In December 1980, the UN General Assembly resolved that, because of its inhumane policies of apartheid, "all states [should] take steps to prevent all cultural, academic, sports, and other exchanges with the racist regime of South Africa." In response to Botha's martial law agenda, both the United Nations and the United States came down hard. In 1986, the UN Security Council strengthened its 1977 arms embargo. In September 1986, the US Congress passed the Comprehensive Anti-Apartheid Act, listing trade items to be boycotted and prohibiting new US investment, sales to the police and military, and new bank loans.

The United States especially was alive with talk of divestment, that is, ceasing to invest in companies that traded with or had operations in South Africa. The leaders of most Western nations, including US president Ronald Reagan, and some leaders of the anti-apartheid movement in South Africa vigorously opposed such action, arguing that it would make the economic realities of all South Africans much worse. But it was the horrors and evils of apartheid that gave rise to the quite populist US rejection campaign. The leaders were college and university students and faculty. By 1988, 155 American colleges had at least partially cast off investments. The University of California alone deprived the South African government of an investment of $3.1 billion; this massive amount, Nelson Mandela contended, was especially significant in ending South African white-minority rule.[14] On Mandela's birthday, July 18, the University of California Regents voted 13–9 for full divestment of the system's $3.1 billion linked to South Africa through US corporations and banks. Part of this new effort resulted from student memories of the effects of apartheid, specifically the brutality of the Soweto killings, Biko's assassination, and the forced resettlement of blacks in designated "reservations." In the spring of 1986, University of California at Berkeley was the site of shantytown construction and militant protests that dramatically raised the political cost of continued University of California investment tied to South Africa.

By the end of the 1980s, twenty-six states, twenty-two counties, and ninety cities in the United States had either partially or completely withdrawn their investments; from 1985 to 1990, more than two hundred US corporations had stripped away $1 billion from South Africa's economy. As businesses, investors, and money left the country, this capital flight wreaked havoc on South Africa's economy, giving rise to double-digit inflation. The economic situation only heightened the growing anti-apartheid fervor.

On August 15, 1985, P. W. Botha gave a speech at the National Party (the white government party congress). At the conference Botha was expected to change his negative take on apartheid in the country as he saw it. He did nothing of the sort, instead emphasizing apartheid as the path to the future. Botha spoke: "From certain international as well as local quarters, appeals are being made to me to release Mr. Nelson Mandela from jail. . . .But let me remind the public . . . why Mr. Mandela is in jail . . . the accused deliberately and maliciously plotted and engineered the commission of acts of violence and destruction throughout the country. The planned purpose thereof was to bring about . . . chaos, disorder, and turmoil. The saboteurs had planned the manufacture of at least seven types of bombs [including] 48,000 anti-personnel mines, 210,000 hand grenades. . . . We, who are committed to peaceful negotiation. . . have a warning to them: . . . our readiness to negotiate should not be mistaken for weakness.[15]

Botha saw anti-apartheid blacks, including Mandela, as creators of disorder, chaos, and turmoil, just as Deng Xiaoping saw the Tiananmen demonstrators moving toward rebellion and violent insurrection. Botha's last warning suggested a common misunderstanding of any enemy as someone who would only respond to strength, power, and brute force. Deng conveyed the same message bluntly: "Clear the Square." It was a most common reaction of dictatorial elites to anyone who dared challenge them or provide alternative measures. This situation did not seemingly bode well for the future.

CHAPTER 7

Written on the Darkest Pages of Human History, 1991–2000

In a judgment pertaining to the 1995 Srebrenica genocide, Fouad Riad, an Egyptian judge on the UN's International Criminal Tribunal for the former Yugoslavia (ICTY), wrote that the incident was "written on the darkest pages of human history."[1] He spoke of the 1995 Bosnian genocide, reflecting on one historical episode, but his judgment can be taken as a more general comment on the history of the 1990s. What we see on these dark pages of history, written in blood, are accounts of war, massacres, mass rape, genocide, terrorism, ethnic cleansing, and assassination. The tragic situations were worsened by insufficient and laggard responses and strategic disagreements and indecisiveness on the part of the UN and key leaders of Western nations. The result was policy paralysis, which only exacerbated the bloodbaths of the Bosnian genocide (1995), the Rwandan genocide (1994), and the two Congo Wars (1996–1997 and 1998–2003).

But emerging from that enshrouding darkness came bright beacons that illuminated not only the 1990s but also the whole of the twentieth century: the most splendid was the end of apartheid in South Africa. When F. W. de Klerk became president in September 1989, he realized that, given South Africa's precarious international position and the possibility of civil war, rapid reform was mandatory. He revoked some segregationist laws that separated black and whites in public places. In 1990, he freed Nelson Mandela after twenty-seven years in prison, removed restrictions on political groups, and legalized the African National Congress (ANC), which, for its part, ended its armed struggle against Pretoria's government. After negotiations with the ANC about transforming South Africa into a racially integrated democracy, the government in June 1991 repealed the last legal foundations for apartheid

The Twentieth Century: A World History. Keith Schoppa, Oxford University Press. © Oxford University Press 2021.
DOI: 10.1093/oso/9780190497354.003.0008

and called for a new constitution. De Klerk's "revolution," immediately following Botha's racist extremes, underscores the importance of the individual in historical change.

In December 1993, Mandela and de Klerk were co-winners of the Nobel Prize for Peace. In his Nobel speech Mandela graciously thanked the millions around the globe involved in the anti-apartheid movement: "Because of their courage and persistence . . . we can join together to celebrate one of the outstanding human victories of our century. I am here today [partly] as a representative of the millions of people across the globe supporting the anti-apartheid movement. Both inside and outside our country, they had the nobility of spirit to stand in the path of tyranny and injustice, without seeking selfish gain."[2]

In the early 1990s, De Klerk spearheaded fundamental reforms in South Africa institutions and processes to set up the ending of apartheid. De Klerk summed up the process of his negotiations in 1990–1991: "The driving force . . . was a fundamental change of heart. It was . . . a process of realization of the futility of ongoing conflict; acknowledgement of failed policies and the injustice it brought with it, not by external pressure, but primarily by social changes which economic growth generated."[3] Mandela was inaugurated the first black president of South Africa and de Klerk, his first deputy.

Author Nadine Gordimer was in the Pretoria courtroom in 1964 when Mandela received a life sentence for subversion against the state; indeed, she edited his three-hour self-defense speech ("I Am Prepared to Die"). She joined the outlawed ANC, became an active member, and even hid ANC leaders in her home. Gordimer spoke out at home and abroad against apartheid and political repression. She was one of the first people Mandela asked to see after his release from prison. In 1991, she won the Nobel Prize for Literature for her collection of novels and short stories "tackling 'human tensions of life' during apartheid."

The two Nobel laureates gave each other high praise. In his autobiography, Mandela said her writing taught him much about "white liberal sensibility." In a remarkable accolade, Gordimer made Mandela a global symbol for "one of the outstanding human victories of our century." For all the century's scientific, technological, and medical achievements, it was the triumph of the human spirit that most strikingly symbolized the best in the twentieth century—through the lives and work of men and women like Chico Mendes, Mahatma Gandhi, Federico Garcia Lorca, Lu Xun, Mother Teresa, Romeo Dallaire, Wilfred Owen, Alexander Dubcek, Gro Harlem Brundtland, Yitzhak Rabin, John XXIII, Vaclav

Nelson Mandela and F. W. de Klerk collaborated in dismantling apartheid and shared the Nobel Peace Prize for their work. Their working relationship was often strained, but Mandela said, "We might have our occasional disagreements, but we spend all our time working together to attain the ends for what we both believe we should be working." © Sasa Kralj/AP/Shutterstock 7304705A

Havel, and Nelson Mandela. Gordimer defined Mandela in grand and global terms: "He is at the epicenter of our time, ours in South Africa, and, yours, wherever you are."[4]

Israeli-Palestinian relations brought a hopefulness, which, while flickering, showed once again the importance of the individual in making change. Unfortunately, in the end the bright prospect was brutally snuffed out. In 1987, the first Palestinian Intifada ("shaking")—an effort to shake off Israeli power and realize Palestinian independence—involved primarily nonviolent demonstrations and strikes. There were, however, some violent incidents. Serving as defense minister at the time, Yitzhak Rabin, the son of Ukrainian parents, had excelled as a student; his interests turned to the military, where, moving up the ranks quickly, he had an illustrious twenty-seven-year career. As Israeli Defense Forces chief of staff, he directed the successful Six-Day War in June 1967 and served as prime minister (1974–1977 and 1992–1995). In his second term, he endorsed the Israeli-Palestinian peace process.

The government of Norway under Prime Minister Brundtland invited Rabin, his Foreign Minister Simon Peres, and Palestine Liberation Organization (PLO) leader Yasir Arafat to Oslo to discuss peace possibilities. Rabin, it was said, was convinced by the Intifada that the status quo was unsustainable and that something must be done. The Brundtland government brokered what became known as the Oslo Accords, signed by Rabin, Peres, and Arafat in September 1993. A remarkable agreement furthering the peace process, it brought mutual recognition, with Arafat and the PLO recognizing Israel's right to exist. Although it did not create a Palestinian state, it established the Palestinian National Authority with limited self-governance over the Gaza Strip and seven cities on the West Bank (of the Jordan River). For this giant step, Rabin, Peres, and Arafat received the Nobel Peace Prize in 1994; Rabin's Nobel lecture was a moving and poignant statement on decision-making for war, so much at heart a mark of the century:

> Of all the memories I have stored up in my seventy-two years, what I shall remember most, to my last day, are the silences. The heavy silence of the moment after, and the terrifying silence of the moment before. As a military . . . commander, I issued orders for . . . hundreds of military operations. . . . I shall always remember the moment just after making the decision to mount an action: the hush as senior officers or cabinet ministers slowly rise from their seats [to leave the room];. . . the sound of the closing door; and then the silence in which I remain alone. That is the moment you grasp that as a result of the decision just made, people will be going to their deaths. People from my nation, people from other nations. . . . At that hour, they are still laughing and weeping; still weaving plans and dreaming about love; still musing about planting a garden or building a house. . . . Which of them is fated to die? Whose mother will soon be in mourning? Whose world will crumble under the weight of the loss? . . . I will also forever remember the silence of the moment before: the hush . . . when time is running out and in another hour, another minute, the inferno will erupt. In that moment of great tension just before the finger pulls the trigger, just before the fuse begins to burn; in the terrible quiet of that moment, there's still time to wonder, alone: Is it really imperative to act? Is there no other choice? No other way? And then the order is given and the inferno begins.[5]

On November 4, 1995, after a peace rally in Tel Aviv, Rabin was assassinated by an ultra-conservative Jew enraged over the Oslo

Accords. Rabin's courage and determination amid virulent Israeli opposition and death threats, as well as his commitment to peace, made him larger than life for his supporters. His death was a severe setback for peace because his successors, led by an inflexible Benjamin Netanyahu, reverted automatically to the idea of permanent confrontation, and the Oslo Accords died on the vine.

Technological and medical successes brightened the last decade of the century and millennium. Computer science–related inventions dominated the decade's technology, building on the foundation of the information age: advances in the World Wide Web, the invention of Google, the launching of the iMAC (one of the world's most popular desktop computers), the beginnings of Amazon and eBay (two of the biggest online shopping portals), and the invention of mobile devices and digital phones. In biological research, the International Human Genome project (1990) worked to determine the sequence of chemical base pairs that constituted human DNA; the ultimate goal: identifying and mapping all the genes of the human genome from both physical and functional standpoints. Completed in 2003, it offered the eventual possibility of better diagnosis and treatment of diseases. In 1998, came the isolation of human embryonic stem cells, cells capable of continually reproducing themselves and regenerating all cells in the human body, an especially exciting finding for transplantation medicine. But the origin of these cells in human embryos or fetal tissue made the question of "harvesting" them an ethical one. The practice of cloning took on an new immediacy when, in 1996, Dolly, a cloned sheep, was born, genetically identical to a six-year-old ewe. The ethical implications: If sheep could be successfully cloned, why not human beings? That possibility raised profound questions about interpreting human life and especially, in light of this study, about the nature of identity and individuality.

Now we go into the dark, first with the collapse of the federated nation of Yugoslavia and its aftermath. After communist dictator Josip Broz Tito's death in 1980, ethnic tensions rose in those countries making up Yugoslavia (Bosnia-Herzegovina, Croatia, Serbia, Slovenia, and Montenegro). If each ethnic group had been situated within one bounded territory, the situation might have been less unstable. But instead there were enclaves of all the ethnic groups in each country, creating a tinderbox, with the ongoing potential of flaming quickly into a conflagration. In addition, the 1974 constitution gave Yugoslavia's republics the right to regulate their public affairs independently, immediately starting a power drain from the federal government to the republics.

In Slovenia, political liberalization had begun in 1984, and, as the decade ended, calls for independence from Yugoslavia grew louder, with Croatia joining those calls. In independence referenda, 88.5 percent of Slovenes and 93.2 percent of Croats voted for independence. In March 1991, several months before Croatia declared its independence, the Yugoslav army invaded, laying an eight-month siege on Dubrovnik and its environs. Though the Croats won in the end, the war (1991–1995), brought by Serbia and Croatian Serbs, killed at least twenty thousand, displaced about five hundred thousand refugees, and devastated the country's infrastructure. During the war both Serbs and Croats laid two million landmines in no particular pattern and with no record of their placement. In 2011, there were still a hundred towns and districts studded with unexploded mines that killed or injured at least nineteen hundred people since 1991.

Both Croatia and Slovenia declared independence on June 25, 1991. Two days later, Serbian President Slobodan Milosevic, acting as ruler of Yugoslavia, dispatched the Yugoslav army to Slovenia, where it made a lackluster attempt to forestall Slovenia's independence (the "Ten-Day War"). In the end, Milosevic decided its independence did not much matter because, unlike Croatia, there were not many Serbs in Slovenia.

The first campaign in the Bosnian War (1992–1996) was the longest siege of a capital city, Sarajevo, in modern warfare's history: 1,425 days from April 5, 1992, to February 29, 1996. Serb and Bosnian Serb forces positioned themselves on heights surrounding the city, pounding the capital with deadly bombings of civilian sites (twice at a large city market) and sniping civilians along its streets, killing over ten thousand people. In April 1992, Bosnia-Herzegovina (BH), acting without the Bosnian Serbs, proclaimed its independence, a declaration that spurred immediate attacks on Bosnia's Muslim areas. The Serbs' goal was to establish a Serb state, Republika Srpska, mapped as an arc from BH's north, through Serbia, to Montenegro and Kosovo on its south. This meant annexing mostly Muslim lands in eastern Bosnia, which would of necessity undergo ethnic cleansing.

The UN and leaders of key Western nations disagreed on strategies for forestalling ethnic cleansing and ending the war.[6] In the aftermath of its tragic 1993 humanitarian mission in Mogadishu, Somalia, the United States chose not to send peacekeeping troops to the Balkans. Instead, Washington urged NATO to contain the Serbs and Bosnian Serbs through bombing. But key allies, Great Britain and France, opposed bombing because their own troops, whose UN mandate was humanitarian, were then at risk participating in UN peacekeeping operations on the ground.

In April 1993, the UN Security Council declared six towns "safe areas," which UN peacekeepers were to protect from armed attack.[7] However, the Security Council refused to authorize enough troops to defend these areas. Secretary-General Boutros-Ghali had requested 37,000 men, but Western nations protested and dropped the number to 7,600 (a drop of 80 percent from what Boutros-Ghali had asked for, providing only 1,267 soldiers per safe area). The UN's mission as peacekeepers meant maintaining neutrality and even-handedness in dealing with both sides in the war; it did not mean actively opposing Serb aggression and siding with their Muslim victims. Here the UN mission did not fit with the reality of Serbia's utter contempt for the international laws of war.

Air strikes to block or at least slow Serb advances were crucial; however, after a May 25, 1995, strike, the Serbs took 370 UN troops hostage. In response, NATO refused to send any more air strikes, in effect giving the Bosnian Serbs a green light to proceed. In the Serb crosshairs was Srebrenica, a salt-mining town that they had besieged from April 1992. Its population of less than ten thousand was roughly 75 percent Muslim and 25 percent Serbian. By July 1995, the population had soared to about forty thousand with incoming Muslim refugees. Even before the May 25 air strike, the commander of UN troops on the ground, French General Bernard Janvier, called on the Security Council to cede the "safe areas" outright to the Bosnian Serbs since they were "indefensible."[8] On July 8, the UN Dutch commander in Srebrenica requested close air support as the Bosnian Serb attack seemed imminent. UN British Commander Lt. General Rupert Smith in Sarajevo refused, saying, "It's too early and not worth the risk."[9]

Three days later, five thousand Bosnian Serb troops invaded Srebrenica under command of Bosnian Serb General Ratko Mladic; about three hundred UN peacekeeping Dutch soldiers were the total "protecting" the town. The Bosnian Serb plan was to kill all civilian Muslim males from fifteen to sixty-five years old and to forcibly deport women, children, and the elderly to other Muslim areas (before which many women were raped). The UN Dutch soldiers actually collaborated with the Serbs, in effect supporting their actions. Several hundred Srebrenicans sought refuge in the UN compound, but the Dutch expelled them as the Serbs neared. They then helped the Serbs separate the men and boys from the others. Between July 11 and 13, 8,373 Muslim males were loaded onto trucks, taken to the sites where they were massacred, and then bulldozed into mass graves. The UN provided thirty thousand liters of gasoline to fuel the transport of men

A Muslim father grieves over the grave of his son in Bosnia-Herzegovina in May 1994. The father and his two other sons have their hands outstretched with their palms up, a Muslim practice in prayer. This area endured the vicious ethnic cleansing of Bosnian Muslims by Croats. UN Photo 78969

and boys to their executions and bulldozers to plough the mass graves. NATO air strikes began again in September, fully two months after the Srebrenica tragedy.

Srebrenica had been "ethnically cleansed": there were no Bosnian Muslims (Bosniaks) left in the town. The ICTY classified it as genocide: the largest mass murder in the most devastating military conflict in Europe since World War II. Estimates of those killed in Bosnia totaled about 200,000, with 20,000 to 50,000 women raped and 2.2 million refugees displaced. Altogether 160 men and one woman were indicted for war crimes and crimes against humanity in Bosnia; of these, 14 were indicted for the Srebrenica genocide. Mladic was charged with war crimes, crimes against humanity, and two counts of genocide (for his actions in Sarajevo and Srebrenica). He was found guilty and sentenced to life in prison. Radovan Karadzik, head of Republika Srpska, was sentenced to forty years in prison. In a critical 1999 review of the Bosnian catastrophe, then UN secretary-general Kofi Annan (who had been in charge of UN peacekeeping operations in 1995) wrote: "Through error, misjudgment, and the inability to recognize the scope of evil confronting us, we failed to do our part to save the people of Srebrenica from the Serb campaign of mass murder."[10] He believed that the Srebrenica tragedy would haunt the history of the UN forever.

Leaders of Western nations dilatorily muddled along through the Bosnian tragedy until the Srebrenica genocide shocked them into the bombing strategy that ended the war with the Dayton Accords in a matter of only three months. This peace agreement was signed by the presidents of Bosnia, Croatia, and Serbia on November 21, 1995, at an airbase near Dayton, Ohio: hence the name of the Accords. It ended the war in Bosnia and outlined a General Framework Agreement for Peace in Bosnia and Herzegovina. It preserved Bosnia as a single state made up of two parts, the Bosniak-Croat federation and the Bosnian Serb Republic. Sarajevo continued as the undivided capital city.

Slobodan Milosevic, president of Serbia from 1989 to 1997 and the Federal Republic of Yugoslavia from 1997 to 2000, was indicted for war crimes, not for his actions in the Bosnian War, but in the Kosovo War (1998–1999). While he assisted in the Dayton Accords, he moved, in the end, to create a "Greater Serbia"—to combine Republika Srpska with Montenegro and Kosovo (a province of Serbia until 2008). Milosevic's Kosovo plan involved making the Serbs the majority by ethnically cleansing Albanians, the majority ethnic group, who wanted independence from Serbia. Championing his Serb nationalistic identity, Milosevic dispatched Serb troops into Kosovo. The pattern of Bosnian War crimes was replicated in Kosovo (1998–1999) with Serb soldiers ethnically cleansing Albanians. His trial began in 2001; it was ongoing when he died of a heart attack in March 2006.

In eastern Africa, the bad blood and open hostility between Hutus and Tutsis did not abate after the Tutsi genocide of the Hutus in 1972. A peace agreement in August 1993 ending a two-year civil war (1990–1992) between the Hutus and Tutsis established a broad-based transitional government. The UN established UNAMIR (UN Assistance Mission in Rwanda) to oversee the execution of the peace agreement; UNAMIR was lightly armed and had no military mandate. General Romeo Dallaire, the Canadian commander of UNAMIR, was a career military officer who repeatedly pleaded the UN for more troops, ammunition, and equipment, and—in January 1994—for the authority to seize Hutu arms caches. The UN denied all his requests. He asked the United States to block Hutu radio transmissions ratcheting up hatred of the Tutsis, but the answer was no. His cable in January warned of the risk of genocide; Kofi Annan received it but did not share it with the Security Council or follow up in any way.

On April 6, 1994, the presidents of Rwanda and Burundi (both Hutus) were killed when their plane was shot down near Kigali Airport in the Rwandan capital. Their assassinations were the pretext for Hutu extremists to begin a genocidal war the very next day against the Tutsis, whom the Hutus disparaged as "cockroaches." For one hundred days Rwanda was drenched in blood: eight hundred thousand to one million Tutsis and politically moderate Hutus were murdered. In Burundi, the civil war–genocide cost three hundred thousand lives. The "hundred days" produced two million refugees.

Despite this bleakness, a star of UNAMIR was Mbaye Diagne, a courageous and conscientious Senegalese military officer, who served as UN military observer. One of nine children born to a family living near Dakar, he was the first in his family to attend college. In Rwanda, although it was beyond his UN duties, he was credited with saving from six hundred to one thousand lives through almost continual rescue missions at great danger to himself. Considered a true African hero, he often had to pass with those he was trying to save through multiple risky checkpoints manned by Hutu killers. At these times, he benefited from his previous contacts with the military and from his innate ability to defuse tense situations by using humor in off-the-cuff jokes. According to Gregory Alex, the head of the UN Humanitarian Assistance team, and a friend, he told his jokes and satirical remarks "with the smile, a big toothy grin."[11] He was ready in friendly conversation to bribe checkpoint guards, if need be, with money, cigarettes, and alcohol. He was killed instantly at age thirty-six on May 31, 1994, when a mortar shell exploded behind his jeep and sent shrapnel into the back of his head. In speaking of his death, Dallaire said, "It was a very difficult day . . . we lost one of those shining lights, one of those beacon-type guys who influences others. He had a sense of humanity that went well beyond orders, well beyond any mandate." In May 2014, the UN Security Council created the Captain Mbaye Diagne Medal for Exceptional Courage.[12]

Before the genocide began, UNAMIR had 2,548 troops, but three weeks into the twelve-week killing spree, the Security Council unanimously slashed the number of troops to 270. Eventually realizing that colossal mistake, it later raised the number to 5,500, a goal not reached until late November: the UN had no troops of its own; and in this hellish situation, the UN had difficulty getting member nations to offer more troops. All in all, the UN's mission was bungled.

Reports from UNAMIR were often ignored. The Security Council was not given information about what was really happening in Rwanda and did not seem committed to the effort. There were continual delays on the UN's part. Kofi Annan, in charge of UN Peacekeeping at the time, took actions or failed to take actions that bordered on dereliction of duty. Once the killing started, Western leaders did not respond, revealing a lack of interest or political will or sheer ignorance or malignant racism. The US ambassador to Rwanda dismissed the slaughter as "tribal killings." The US deputy assistant secretary of state reported, "I was told . . . that these people do this from time to time."[13] In Dallaire's judgment: "The world is racist. Africans don't count; Yugoslavians do. More people were killed, injured, . . . and refugeed in one hundred days in Rwanda than in [all the years] of the Yugoslav campaign. . . . Why didn't the world come? Because there was no self-interest. . . . They didn't come because some humans are [considered] less than human."[14]

Dallaire returned to Canada in August 1994 and received senior military appointments. But he suffered from severe post-traumatic stress disorder (PTSD), sinking into a deep despair that led to multiple suicide attempts. He was released from the military in 2000 for medical reasons. Serving as senator in the Canadian Parliament from 2005 to 2014, he became a voice of conscience for global humanitarianism.

During and after the genocide, an estimated two million refugees, mostly Hutu, poured over Rwanda's western border into eastern Zaire (the name by which the Congo had been known from 1971 to 1997). Refugee camps morphed into de facto military bases for refugee Hutus, who terrorized and robbed the local population. A Congolese Tutsi's uprising to force the Rwandans back to Rwanda in October 1996 ignited the first Congo War (October 1996–May 1997). In response, Rwanda, Burundi, and Uganda sent armies into Zaire to liberate it from military dictator Joseph Mobutu and to install Laurent Kabila as head of the Alliance of Democratic Forces. Mobutu was overthrown in May 1997, and Kabila became president of the renamed Democratic Republic of Congo (DRC) in September.

The size of Western Europe, the DRC was mired in poverty, even though it was resource rich, with gold, diamonds, copper, cobalt, and zinc. Kabila's decision to allow Hutus to regroup in eastern DRC antagonized his former supporters, Rwanda and Uganda. That prompted them into a 1998 joint invasion in which they supported rebels against Kabila while Angola, Namibia, and Zimbabwe sided with Kabila. This second Congo War (1998–2003), called the "great war of Africa," was fought by nine African countries plus about twenty-five separate armed groups.

Rwandans crowd the Ndosha refugee camp on the border between Rwanda and Zaire. The date is July 25, 1994, ten days after the horrific genocide of Tutsis and moderate Hutus by Rwandan extremists. This was a special refugee camp for children and the young whose parents were killed in the genocide, and it operated for more than three years. Note the young boy in the foreground; his face does not mask well the disappointment and fear with which he accompanied the refugees. UN Photo 78969

It was one of the ten deadliest wars in history and the world's deadliest since World War II: six million perished, many from disease and starvation. A heinous tragedy of the war was the mass rape of females of all ages and of men and boys as well: Amnesty International tallied forty thousand cases of rape. Inside the DRC 3.4 million were displaced, and 2 million became refugees in Burundi, Rwanda, Tanzania, Uganda, and Zambia. The Mbuti pygmies in the DRC's northeast were especially targeted. One survivor told the UN's Indigenous People's Forum that the Mbutis were hunted down and eaten as if they were game animals. Both sides of the war viewed them as subhuman and useless.

The war and its horrors were vastly underreported; like the UN's and Western leaders' lack of attention and response, most people not in Africa did not even know it was happening. Suggested reasons for this ignorance and apathy are that the DRC was remote and impenetrable; it played little role in world affairs; despite its huge mineral deposits, it had no real geostrategic importance; and, crucially and tragically, blatant anti-black racism ran rampant among much global media, some world political leaders, and many of the world's people.

The UN declared 1993 the International Year of the World's Indigenous Peoples in order to "strengthen international cooperation for solving [their] problems." In the late 1990s, there were 370 million indigenous peoples in seventy countries—about 5 percent of the world's population yet making up 15 percent of the poorest. For the people of Australia, the Sydney Olympics in 2000 was a reawakening to the plight of indigenous peoples, specifically Australian aborigines, who had been harshly mistreated by Australian governments in the past. The Olympic cauldron was lit by Cathy Freeman, a twenty-seven-year-old short-distance runner who was an indigenous Australian. Winning gold in the 400-meter event, Freeman ran her victory lap carrying both the aboriginal and Australian flags, a choice seen as a symbol of hope for a country coming to terms with the legacy of its wrenching assimilation policies. From 1910 to 1970, these policies were targeted to absorb aboriginal people into white society through the hard-to-stomach process of removing at least one hundred thousand children from their families. The ultimate goal was to destroy aboriginal society. With that goal in mind, as the "Stolen Generation" was forcibly taken from their parents and uprooted from their families, records as to their actual parentage and the dates and places of their births were pointedly destroyed, a process some have called "sanitized cultural genocide." Cathy Freeman's grandmother was one of the Stolen Generation; Freeman noted that she herself was very upset when John Howard, the prime minister from 1996 to 2007, refused to make a formal apology to the Stolen Generation, though his successor publicly apologized in February 2008. One newspaper described Freeman's role at the Olympics: "The hope of a whole nation had been pinned on her performance which was seen by many as a symbol of reconciliation: black and white united in pride and spirit."[15] Yet two decades later, efforts to grant aborigines constitutional recognition, to deal with continuing discrimination against them, to maintain budgets for health benefits and legal aid—*all have failed*, wrapped up in an obnoxious argument that "people have the right to be bigots." Olympic hope turned to ashes!

Whereas 24 nations participated in the 1900 Olympic games, 199 nations did so in 2000—a statistic that underscores the increased globalization throughout the century. At the turn of the twenty-first century, "globalization" became a term both celebrated and maligned for its meaning and impacts. Protests in Washington, DC, in April 2000 and in Prague in September 2000 against the International Monetary Fund and the World Bank revealed an incipient backlash against globalization, seen by some to be the implacable foe of nationalism. A strong advocate for globalization and vigorous critic of nationalism, the 2010 Nobel Prize winner in Literature, Peruvian Mario Vargas Llosa, claimed that nationalism held everyone who lived in that nation captive, living boxed into a powerful ideological conformity. In his Nobel speech, he declared that

> nationalism [is] the incurable plague of the modern world. . . I despise every form of nationalism, a provincial ideology—or rather, religion—that is short-sighted, exclusive, that cuts off the intellectual horizon and hides in its bosom ethnic and racist prejudices, for it transforms into a supreme value, the fortuitous circumstance of one's birthplace. Along with religion, nationalism has been the cause of the worst slaughters in history.[16]

In retrospect, the twentieth century was the most flagrantly violent of any in history. Although totaling the exact numbers of deaths due to fighting, genocide, refugee flight, and disease is impossible, the best estimates of the century's war-related deaths totaled about 187 million. Scholars suggest two reasons for the twentieth century's uniquely lethal concatenation of violence. In wars waged before the twentieth century, there had been deep-seated technological, political, and social limitations that ultimately held down death rates; but in the twentieth century all such limits were off. Massacres and (worse) genocides became shockingly common. Second, leaders and heads of state, presiding over seemingly civilized polities, were able to unloose the most primal homicidal and barbarous inclinations of their people.[17] Terrorist attacks of the 1990s, though generally smaller in scale than those in the twenty-first century, were but harbingers of more fearsome terrorist threats in the twenty-first century.

The life and career of Aung San Suu Kyi offer insights into issues related to identity—what she stood for, how she saw herself, and how she appeared to others. In addition, her choices dealing with identity bring into play the three social-political levels or tiers that vie for our attention in the postmodern world: the individual, the nation, and the international or global. She was the daughter of Aung San, the "father" of the modern nation of Myanmar. Suu Kyi, educated at Delhi University and Oxford University, was influenced by Gandhi's ideas on nonviolence and by Buddhist concepts such as the emphasis on compassion.

After graduating from Oxford, she worked on global issues at the United Nations for three years. She had married Michael Aris, a Tibetan scholar, in 1972 and had given birth to two sons, Alexander in 1973 and Kim in 1977. She returned to Myanmar in 1988 to care for her ailing mother.

That same year, she urged Myanmar's military junta to establish democracy, a proposal for which she was placed under house arrest in July 1989. During fifteen of the next twenty-one years, she remained there, the most prominent political prisoner in the world. Global protests were loud and continuous. She won the respect of the masses for her loyalty to her homeland and her solidarity with prisoners for the cause of democracy. Finally freed in 2010, she was elected to Parliament in 2012; after her party's sweeping victory in November 2015, she became state counselor—de facto prime minister.

Suu Kyi's identity, platform, and high-minded moral principles had always placed her in the highest ranks of human rights supporters in the global community. But then a problem appeared that turned Suu Kyi's identity on its head and raised many questions. Myanmar was 89 percent Buddhist and only 4.2 percent Muslim; the Myanmar Buddhists discriminated against all Muslims, but most especially they bitterly despised the ethnic Rohingya, in a conspicuous display of outright dehumanization. As examples, the government formally denied the Rohingyas citizenship; they were treated as illegal immigrants brought in by Britain and not entitled to government protection. Their government deprived them of health services, any relief aid or assistance, the right to worship and to move freely, and the right to education (the Rohingya literacy rate in 2017 was only 20 percent). There were restrictions on owning property, the right to marry, and limits on the number of children couples could have (only two); if they had any more, they could be imprisoned and their children blacklisted.

In August 2017, an insurgent Rohingya group launched attacks on twenty-four Myanmar police posts, killing seventy-one officers. The Myanmar army and government reacted with what they and Suu Kyi euphemistically called a "counter-terrorism" campaign. That military campaign gave rise to charges of genocide—war crimes, mass rapes and killings, torture, the arson destruction of 288 separate villages, and the flight of 700,000 Rohingya refugees, most to nearby Bangladesh. The UN High Commissioner on Human Rights called it in a speech at Geneva, "a textbook example of ethnic cleansing."[18]

Did Nobel laureate Suu Kyi, spokeswoman for human rights and democracy, act to stop the attacks on human rights and set a more positive path to democracy? No, she did essentially nothing. She would not acknowledge the political, economic, and social discrimination or the immense disadvantages that the Rohingya faced. She even refused to say the word "Rohingya." She said that the only problem that had to be dealt with was "terrorism." She did not note the army's own terrorism in dealing with the situation. In her defense, she neither controlled the military nor was it accountable to her; it acted with impunity. Perhaps, given the army's power, she thought it unwise for the country if she rattled military cages. In any event, she never seemed to try to use her moral authority to shape or stem the tide of events. As one critic said, "The moral opprobrium that now attaches to her constitutes a reversal of fortunes that verges on tragedy."[19]

Suu Kyi, imprisoned in her home, had carried the flame of democracy and human rights. But now she was silent, though not neutral in the army-Rohingya fight. She had chosen her side; she had chosen her identity: the army that she had held in contempt for many years now became her colleagues and those with whom she most linked herself.

U2 singer and humanitarian Bono presented the Burmese leader Aung San Suu Kyi with Amnesty International's Ambassador of Conscience award in 2012 in recognition of her work in support of human rights. Amnesty International withdrew the award in response to her support for the Myanmar military's genocide against the Rohingya Muslims in 2016–2017. PA Images/Alamy Stock Photo G596D5

Her decision reflected an exaltation of Myanmar/Buddhist nationalism and a barely hidden Islamophobia. The international community was outraged. Almost four hundred thousand people signed petitions to the Nobel Prize committee asking that her prize be stripped from her; according to the rules, that was not possible. The US Holocaust Memorial Museum, however, did rescind its 2012 Elie Wiesel Award because of "her refusal to stop or condemn military violence against the Muslim Rohingya minority."[20] In 2012 Amnesty International had given Suu Kyi its highest honor, the Ambassador of Conscience Award; in 2018, it revoked that award "in light of [her] shameful betrayal of the values she once stood for." "Today we are profoundly dismayed that [she] no longer represents a symbol of hope, courage, and the undying defense of human rights," said Kumi Naidoo, secretary general of Amnesty International.[21]

Suu Kyi had changed markedly in identity and outlook from late 2015 on; from championing human rights to thumbing her nose at human rights (specifically, supporting the jailing of Reuters journalists who were simply reporting the news), from continually fighting the military oligarchy to siding with those same generals in the Rohingya genocide and commenting that they were really "rather sweet."[22] Certainly, context had much to do with her identity change. No longer was Suu Kyi on the "outs" with the government, now she was an important part of that government. One might suggest that she took the stand she did for political or philosophical reasons; that may well be true. But her decisions aligned herself with former enemies, whose positions and actions she was constantly rationalizing. On her own calculations, she clearly selected her new identity, yet why she made these choices is unknown. "Why" is always the most puzzling and frustrating question about identity, a question for which we may never find *any* answer, much less *the right* answer.

Suu Kyi's fixation was the nation, which her father had created and for which she lived. She decided not to return to the United Kingdom, where her family was, even when her husband became terminally ill. Through her own choice she did not see her sons grow up, nor did she see her husband from 1995 through his death from prostate cancer in 1999. She did not visit her sons or embrace her dying husband (that is, tend to her needs as an individual) because she feared that the military authorities would refuse to let her back into Myanmar. "When confronted with the choice between nation and family, she had chosen the nation."[23]

Even though for the majority of her mid-adult life—from 1989 to 2010 when she was under house arrest—she attracted the acclaim and respect of the global community, as she became a symbol of what a democratic world focused on human rights might herald, how significant in actuality was "global" to her? It was hard to know at that time. But her dismissive reaction to the global community during the Myanmar genocide of the Rohingya suggests that the nation itself, not the individual or the global, mattered much more in the end.

When she won the Nobel Prize for Peace in 1991, the Myanmar military government refused to let her attend the ceremonies; her eldest son received the award for her. In her Nobel speech, which she finally gave in 2012, Suu Kyi summed up in a personal, poignant, and persuasive way the dramatic tragedy of the twentieth century.

> The First World War represented a terrifying waste of youth and potential, a cruel squandering of the positive forces of our planet. The poetry of that era had a special significance for me because I first read it . . . when I was the same age as many of those young men who had to face the prospect of withering before they had barely blossomed . . . . Youth and love and life perishing forever in senseless attempts to capture nameless, unremembered places. And for what? A century on, we have yet to find a satisfactory answer.

And we would ask Suu Kyi a follow-up question in light of the situation in Myanmar at the beginning of 2020: *What are young Myanmar soldiers and young Rohingya militiamen dying for now?* Is it for the outdated dreams of their fathers or grandfathers? Or is it for the power of those who hold it and dare not risk giving it up once they have tasted it and feasted on it?

Or is this the beginning of yet another story? Though in November 2020, Aung San Suu Kyi won 396 out of 476 seats in the combined lower and upper houses of Parliament, her "honeymoon" with the military appointees (which, according to the military-drafted constitution of 2008, must constitute 25 percent of Parliament) was short-lived. Suu Kyi was detained by the military under house arrest in the national capital, Naypyitaw, on February 1, 2021. The military announced that they had taken control of Myanmar for one year, with power lying in the hands of the country's top military commander.

Memories, of course, went back to Suu Kyi's last house arrest from 1989 to 2010. A similar sentence would leave her at ninety-six years of age, and for what? Her view of the young was actually bleak and dark: they had to face the prospect of withering before they had barely

In a century marked by violence, war, and genocide, this sculptural peace symbol now stands in the UN's Visitors Plaza in New York City. Called Non-Violence, it is a bronze replica of a revolver whose barrel is tied into a knot, making the gun unusable. A gift to the United Nations from Luxembourg in 1988, it is the work of Swedish artist Carl Fredrik Reuterswärd. UN Photo #31385/Permission granted from the Non-Violence Project Foundation

blossomed. And (worst thought ever!) they perished forever in senseless attempts to capture nameless, unremembered places. The base of their happiness was uncertain and unclear. Withering and perishing: with all her ideals and hopes she seemed because of people's actions and manipulations to be pulled back into dark situations and perplexities.

In a century marked by violence, war, and genocide, a sculptural peace symbol was placed in the United Nation's Visitors Plaza in New York City. Called *Non-Violence*, it is a bronze sculpture "of an oversized Colt Python .357 Magnum revolver, with its muzzle tied in a knot," making the gun unusable. A gift to the United Nations from Luxembourg in 1988, it is the work of Swedish artist and sculptor Carl Fredrik Reuterswärd. The artist, a friend of John Lennon, noted that the sculpture was designed out of his grief at Lennon's murder in December 1980.

In terms of issues in this book, of course, it is John Lennon's and Yoko Ono's "Imagine," published in 1971, that is most appropriate—at least in its second stanza; there it deals with huge problems that produce fighting and wars, particularly nationalism and religion. "Imagine" has been judged the most influential song of the twentieth century; in 2005, the Canadian Broadcasting Corporation named it the greatest song in the past one hundred years; and in 2017, the United States National Publishers' Association named it the "song of the century." Whether it can bear all these accolades is uncertain.

But perhaps it is the judgment of Kofi Annan, the none-too-effective UN secretary-general during the Balkan genocides, that seems most perceptive of the meaning of the knotted-up gun:

> It has enriched the consciousness
> of humanity with a powerful symbol
>   that encapsulates, in a few simple curves,
>   the greatest prayer of man;
> which asks not for victory, but for peace.

Acknowledgments

The most important person in my effort to bring new eyes to the history of the twentieth century and to mold the new shapes that then appeared was Vice President and Executive Editor of Oxford University Press Nancy Toff, who, as I wended my way through the book exhibits at one of the standard scholarly conventions, called me over and asked me to write a book entitled *The Twentieth Century: A World History*. I was taken somewhat aback by the request, since I was no notable scholar of world history, but in the end I said yes, recognizing a potential great challenge before me in the study of world cultures themselves and the possible number of relevant and stimulating topics that might spin off from my research and writing with exciting, unknown ramifications.

A second important person was Renaissance man Christopher Chantelau, a close personal friend at the time, a skilled musician and a deep thinker who did his own car repairs and remodeled his home. Chris had questions that brought forth my further questions and often reshaped (or started to!) my own thoughts about the material and historical developments. Our lunches were alive with verbal challenges and possible alternatives. He made notable suggestions on the choice of photographs. His advice, whether or not I took it, was important.

A third crucial person who was preeminent in every way was my wife, Beth. She often said she didn't really have any comments on the book material itself, but many times I would ask her opinions about developments or actions in the narrative, and she would answer, usually suggesting something I had not thought of before. Her patience and love were magnificent, especially in the aftermath of my summer accident as I struggled to regain my memory and to "right" myself for finishing the book. From October 2020 until February 2021, she was stellar in helping me with the peculiarities of a cantankerous old lap-top and my often outdated (really feudal) responses to the workings and implications of different technological approaches.

Finally, I must thank those who worked in Nancy's office (most important, she, herself) and her two assistant editors during my book's time, Elizabeth Vaziri and Zara Cannon-Mohammed. I also thank Julia Turner, an employee from Newgen KnowledgeWorks, who worked as the final manuscript was prepared, and all the other editors who worked on parts of the text.

Chronology

JULY 28, 1914–NOVEMBER 11, 1918
World War I (the Great War)

1915–1917
Armenian genocide

NOVEMBER 2, 1917
Balfour Declaration calls for a Jewish homeland in Palestine

NOVEMBER 6–7, 1917
Bolsheviks seize power in Russia

JANUARY 1918–DECEMBER 1920
Spanish flu pandemic

JANUARY–JUNE 1919
Paris Peace Conference; signing of the Treaty of Versailles

DECEMBER 30, 1922
Establishment of the Union of Soviet Socialist Republics (USSR)

1927
Lindbergh's transatlantic flight; first transatlantic telephone call; first "talking" motion picture

1928
Discovery of penicillin, the world's first antibiotic; Jiang Jieshi unites China after the Northern Expedition; Stalin reveals his First Five-Year Plan

OCTOBER 29, 1929
US stock market crash

MARCH–APRIL 1930
Gandhi's Salt March to the sea

1931–1932
Japan seizes Manchuria and makes it a puppet state (Manchukuo)

JANUARY–MARCH 1933
Hitler's rise to dictatorship in Germany

JULY 17, 1936–APRIL 1, 1939
Spanish Civil War

July 7, 1937
Japan invades China, beginning the Sino-Japanese War (1937–1945)

SEPTEMBER 1, 1939
Hitler invades Poland, beginning World War II (1939–1945)

JUNE 22, 1941
Germany invades the USSR

DECEMBER 7, 1941
Japan attacks Pearl Harbor

JUNE 3–7, 1942
Battle of Midway, turning point in the Pacific War

AUGUST 1942
Gandhi leads "Quit India" movement

JUNE 6, 1944
D-Day on Normandy coast

MARCH 9–10, 1945
Massive US firebombing attack kills 100,000 Japanese civilians in Tokyo

AUGUST 6 AND AUGUST 9, 1945
US drops two atomic bombs: on Hiroshima, then Nagasaki

1946–1954
First Indochina War, known in Vietnam as the "French War"

AUGUST 15, 1947
Partition of India

MAY 14, 1948
Israel declared an independent state

OCTOBER 1, 1949
Establishment of the People's Republic of China (PRC)

1954–1968
African American civil rights movement

NOVEMBER 1, 1955–JANUARY 27, 1973
Second Indochina War, known in Vietnam as the "American War"

OCTOBER 4, 1957
USSR launches first artificial satellite, Sputnik

1958–1961
China's Great Leap Forward

1959–1962
In China, the worst famine in human history (Great Famine)

AUGUST 1960–MAY 1989
Sino-Soviet split

1962–1965
Second Vatican Council

October 15–28, 1962
Cuban Missile Crisis

1966–1976
The PRC's Great Proletarian Cultural Revolution

June 28, 1969
Police raid on NYC's Stonewall Inn ignites the gay rights movement

1969–1972
Six manned moon landings under US Apollo project

March 26–December 1971
West Pakistan's genocide against East Pakistan (now Bangladesh)

1975–1979
Cambodian genocide

December 1979–February 1989
Soviet-Afghan War

1980s–1990s
Spread of HIV/AIDS as a global pandemic

1980–1988
Iran-Iraq War

April 26, 1986
Explosion of nuclear reactor at Chernobyl, Ukraine

1989
Tim Berners-Lee announces invention of the World Wide Web

April–June 1989
Tiananmen Square protests in Beijing

1989–1991
Break-up of the Soviet Union

March 31, 1991–December 14, 1995
Croatian War of Independence, ended by Dayton Agreement

June 1991
Legal foundation for apartheid repealed in South Africa

February 7, 1992
Maastricht Treaty signed, creating the European Union

April 5, 1992–December 14, 1995
Bosnian War, ended by Dayton Agreement

April 7, 1994–July 1994
Rwandan genocide

May 10, 1994–June 14, 1999
Nelson Mandela's term as president of South Africa

July 11–13, 1995
Bosnian Serbs' Srebrenica genocide of Bosnian Muslims

March 5, 1998–June 11, 1999
Kosovo War

1998–2003
Second Congo War: "The Great War of Africa"

Notes

INTRODUCTION

1. Jeremy Silvester and Jan-Bart Gewald, *Words Cannot Be Found: German Colonial Rule in Namibia, Annotated Reprint of the 1918 Blue Book* (Leiden: Brill, 2003), 148.

2. Ibid., 71. See Jon M. Bridgman, *The Revolt of the Hereros* (Berkeley: University of California Press, 1981); and Jeremy Sarkin and Carly Fowler, *Reparation for Historical Rights Violation: The International and Historical Dimensions of the Alien Torts Claims Act Genocide Case of the Hereros of Namibia,* Human Rights Review, 2008, 6, Hofstra University School of Law: Legal Studies Research Paper Series. The link between human rights and cattle was found in the more than one thousand words the Herero had to describe the shape and color of the markings. These thousand-plus common words marked the Herero as owners of the cattle. The cattle then figured as human rights property of the Herero.

3. Bruce Vandervort, *Wars of Imperial Conquest in Africa, 1830–1914* (London: Routledge, 1998), 198.

4. Silvester and Gewald, *Words Cannot Be Found*, 116.

5. Ibid., 87.

6. Ibid., 92.

7. Horst Dreschsler, *Let Us Die Fighting: Namibia under the Germans* (n.p.: Lawrence Hill Books, 1981), chap. 2, 17.

8. Silvester and Gewald, *Words Cannot Be Found*, 89–91.

9. Ibid., 87.

10. Ibid., 85.

11. Silvester and Gewald, *Words Cannot Be Found*, 27n28: explained by Dreschsler, *Let Us Die Fighting*, 23. Although a missionary was guiding the negotiations, he, unfortunately, did not explain to the Herero about the German mile.

12. Wolfgang Werner, "A Brief History of Land Dispossession in Namibia," *Journal of Southern African Studies* 19, no. 1 (March 1993): 135.

13. Ibid.

14. Bridgman, *The Revolt of the Hereros,* 67.

15. Tilman Dedering, "A Certain Rigorous Treatment of All Parts of the Nation: The Annihilation of the Herero in German Southwest Africa" (1904), 254; Dedering's writing appears as chap. 10 in Mark Levine and Penny Roberts, eds., *The Massacre in History* (New York: Berghahn Books, Oxford University Press, 1999).

16. Silvester and Gewald, *Words Cannot Be Found*, xxvii.

17. Jeremy Sarkin, *Germany's Genocide of the Herero: Kaiser Wilhelm II, His General, His Settlers, His Soldiers* (Woodbridge, Suffolk, and Rochester, NY: Boydell and Brewer, 2011). See, especially, the chapter, "Did the Kaiser Order the Genocide?," 155–232.

18. Silvester and Gewald, *Words Cannot Be Found*, 108n110.

19. Ibid., 177.

20. Both definitions are in the *Oxford English Dictionary*.

21. See Gizel Hindi, "The Effects of Globalization on Identity," *European Scientific Journal*, Special Edition 1 (June 2014): 531–38.
22. Quote from Emily Fund for a Better World, accessed May 19, 2021, http://www.doonething.org/heroes/pages-b/brundtland-quotes.htm.

CHAPTER 1

1. Henry Adams, *The Education of Henry Adams* (New York: Modern Library, 1918), chap. 25, "The Dynamo and the Virgin" (1900), 382. See www.uh.edu/engines/epi131.htm.
2. Leslie Page Moch, *Moving Europeans: Migration in Western Europe since 1650* (Bloomington: Indiana University Press, 2003), 147.
3. Emmeline Pankhurst and Cicely Hamilton, *Mrs. Pankhurst and the Right to Vote: The History of the Women's Suffrage Movement in Britain* (Paris: Leonaur, 2016). This point of Mrs. Pankhurst's was front and center for all her presentations, pamphlets, propaganda, and livening up her followers. For all its prevalence, it is not written in this biography. Its omnipresence as a crowd-pleaser was, however, written and acclaimed ad nauseum.
4. The account of the reburial ceremony at the Pantheon is recorded, with Francois Mitterand leading the ceremony, in "The Invisible Light," *Journal of the British Society for the History of Radiology* 37 (July 2013): 1–26.
5. "Marie Curie Quotes," BrainyQuote.com, accessed April 3, 2021, https://www.brainyquote.com/authors/marie-curie-quotes. This quotation follows the description of personal adult crisis in one of the most important biographies of Marie Curie: Susan Quinn, *Marie Curie: A Life* (New York: Simon and Schuster, 1995).
6. Edward J. M. Rhoads, *Manchus and Han: Ethnic Relations and Political Power in Late Qing and Early Republican China, 1861–1928* (Seattle: University of Washington Press, 2000), 105.
7. Cited in John Kifner, "Armenian Genocide of 1915: An Overview," *New York Times* archive, 2007, http:www.nytimes.com/ref/timestopics/topics_armeniangenocide.html.
8. Ibid.
9. Jon H. Stallworthy, *The Poems of Wilfred Owen* (London: Chatto and Windus, 1994), 116. All of Owen's works are in the public domain. Before his death, he read in print only five poems that he had written. He never saw any collection of his poetry, nor did he play any role in putting one together.
10. Abdul Rafay Usmani, "The 10 Greatest Military Leaders of All Time," *Odd Historian*, July 31, 2016, https://www.oddhistorian.com/the-10-greatest-military-leaders-of-all-time.
11. Robert Gaudi, *African Kaiser: General Paul von Lettow-Vorbeck and the Great War in Africa, 1914–1918* (New York: Dutton-Caliber, 2017), 2.
12. Peter Gatrell, "Refugees," in 1914–1918 Online: International Encyclopedia of the First World War, ed. Ute Daniel, Peter Gatrell, Oliver Janz, Heather Jones, Jennifer Keene, Alan Kramer, and Bill Nasson (Berlin: Freie Universität Berlin), last updated October 18, 2014, http://encyclopedia.1914-1918-online.net/article/refugees.
13. The material in these two paragraphs comes mainly from David Zabecki, "Military Developments of World War I," in 1914–1918 Online: International Encyclopedia of the First World War, ed. Ute Danile, Peter Gatrell, Oliver Janz, Heather Jones, Jennifer Keene, Alan Kramer, and Bill Nasson (Berlin: Freie Universität Berlin), last updated May 7, 2015, http://encyclopedia.1914-1918-online.net/article/military_developments_of_world_war_i.

14. Neil M. Heyman, *Daily Life during World War I* (Westport, CT: Greenwood Press, 2002), 689–90.

15. Ibid., 111.

16. Wilfred Owen, "Dulce et Decorum Est," Poetry Foundation, accessed May 19, 2021, www.poetryfoundation.org/poems/46560.

17. Ibid.

18. Dominic Hibberd, *Wilfred Owen: A New Biography* (Chicago: Ivan R. Dee, 2003), 20.

CHAPTER 2

1. F. Scott Fitzgerald, *This Side of Paradise* (New York: Charles Scribner's Sons, 1921), 304.

2. Robert Sobel, "Essays, Papers & Addresses: Coolidge and American Business," 1988, Calvin Coolidge Presidential Foundation, 1, accessed May 21, 2021, https://coolidgefoundation.org/resources/essays-papers-addresses-35/.

3. Mary McAuliffe, *When Paris Sizzled: The 1920s Paris of Hemingway, Chanel, Cocteau, Cole Porter, Josephine Baker, and Their Friends* (Lanham, MD: Rowman and Littlefield, 2016), 217.

4. Lu Xun [Hsun], *Selected Stories of Lu Xun [Lu Hsun]* (New York: W. W. Norton, 2003), 18.

5. Barbara Evans Clements, *A History of Women in Russia: From Earliest Time to the Present* (Bloomington: Indiana University Press, 2012), 198.

6. Neues Europa, "Adolf Hitler—Speech to the Reichstag," July 13, 1934, Berlin, Der-Fuehrer.org, accessed on May 21, 2021, http://der-fuehrer.org/reden/english/34-07-13.htm. Hitler spoke to the Reichstag on July 13, 1934, supporting his actions regarding the Night of a Thousand Knives, taken mainly against earlier Nazi stalwarts whom Hitler no longer trusted. This was part of Hitler's moves to complete power, in which he was claiming to do all in his power to benefit the state. This step was followed in two months' time by the Nuremberg Laws.

7. Joseph A. Shumpeter, *Business Cycles: A Theoretical, Historical, and Statistical Analysis of the Capitalist Process* (New York: McGraw-Hill, 1964), 335.

8. "Federico Garcia Lorca Quotes," *Famous Poets and Poems*.com, accessed May 21, 2021, http://famouspoetsandpoems.com/poets/federico_garcia_lorca/quotes.

9. Charles P. Kindleberger, *The World in Depression* (Berkeley: University of California Press, 1986), 112.

10. Federico Garcia Lorca, "Theory and Play of the Duende," Poetry in Translation, 1933, accessed May 21, 2021, http://www.poetryintranslation.com/PITBR/Spanish/LorcaDuende.htm. Although Federico Garcia Lorca associates duende with particular arts like flamenco and bull fighting, he sees its Spanish origins applicable to various elements of Spanish culture. Roughly stated, duende has the "status of mastery achieved by talented practitioners of an art. It is a more aesthetically compelling display of emotion or energy that takes the audience with it, tied together with a sense of fatefulness, of being in touch with both death and life at the same time."

11. Federico Garcia Lorca, *Obras completas*, vol. 2, 20th ed. (Madrid: Aguilar, 1978), 1082–87. Quoted in Ian Gibson, *Federico Garcia Lorca* (New York: Pantheon, 1989), 439.

CHAPTER 3

1. There is debate among historians about whether Franco was truly a fascist. Some have argued that revolutionary elements were important parts of fascism, but

that in Franco's case, his social policy was strictly traditionalist and reactionary. Second, Franco's political action was not based on a popular mass movement, which is typical for a fascist regime. Mihaly Vajda, in *Fascism as a Mass Movement* (Allison & Busby: London, 1976), suggests that rather than fascism Franco's movement was "as an open adversary of revolutionary power" (p. 14); in reality he led a counterrevolution, whose two special bases were Spanish nationalism and reactionary Catholicism.

2. Alejandro Escalona, "75 Years of Picasso's *Guernica*: An Inconvenient Masterpiece," *HuffPost*, July 23, 2012, http://www.huffingtonpost.com/alejandro-escalona/75-years-of-picasso-guernica-b_1538776.html.

3. R. Keith Schoppa, *Revolution and Its Past: Identities and Change in Modern Chinese History*, 4th ed. (Abington, Oxon, UK: Routledge, Francis and Taylor Group, 2020), 236.

4. In the late nineteenth century, Aryan referred to the related group of languages that included Persian, Sanskrit, Greek, Latin, Celtic, and Germanic.

5. The most notable exception was the United Kingdom, which was not projected to become a German province but instead to become an allied seafaring partner of the Germans.

6. Niall Ferguson, *The War of the World: Twentieth-Century Conflict and the Descent of the West* (New York: Penguin Books, 2006), 442.

7. Vesa Nenye, Peter Munter, Toni Wirtanen, and Chris Birks, *Finland at War: The Winter War, 1939–1940* (New York: Bloomsbury, 2015), 17.

8. Richard Bidlack and Nikita Lomagin, *The Leningrad Blockade, 1941–1944: A New Documentary History for the Soviet Union* (New Haven, CT: Yale University Press, 2012), 36.

9. Alan Dowty, *Israel/Palestine* (Cambridge: Cambridge University Press, 2008), 8.

10. Clifton B. Parker, "Jewish Emigres Who Fled Nazi Germany Revolutionized U.S. Science and Technology, Stanford Economist Says," *Stanford Report*, August 11, 2014.

11. Nuclear fission is a process in which the nucleus of an atom is split by a neutron into two or more smaller nuclei, creating much heat energy. It was essential for the creation of nuclear energy as a source of electrical power and for the detonation of weapons.

12. "Henrich Himmler," Death Camps, December 1, 2015, http://www.deathcamps.info/testimonies/Himmler.htm

13. United States Holocaust Memorial Museum, "Documenting Numbers of Victims of the Holocaust and Nazi Persecution," Holocaust Encyclopedia, last edited December 8, 2020, https://encyclopedia.ushmm.org/content/en/article/documenting-numbers-of-victims-of-the-holocaust-and-nazi-persecution; Ina R. Friedman, *The Other Victims: First-Person Stories of Non-Jews Persecuted by the Nazis* (New York: Houghton Mifflin-Harcourt, 1990).

14. The historian is Timothy Snyder in *Bloodlands: Europe between Hitler and Stalin* (New York: Basic Books, 2010).

15. Barbara Hacker Berman, Berman's Branches, accessed May 21, 2021, http://bermansbranches.com/. These are accounts put together by Jewish activists (known as "Berman's branches") who were connected to Jewish public libraries in the Pale of Settlement. See David Shavit, "The Emergence of Jewish Public Libraries in Tsarist Russia," *Journal of Library History* 20, no. 3 (Summer 1985): 239–52.

16. Elie Wiesel, *Night* (New York: Bantam, 1982), 32.

17. Peipei Qiu with Su Zhiliang and Chen Lifei, *Chinese Comfort Women: Testimonies from Imperial Japan's Sex Slaves* (Vancouver: University of British Columbia Press, 2013), 104.

18. Errol Morris, "Film: The Fog of War: Transcript," ErrolMorris.com, accessed May 21, 2021. http://www.errolmorris.com/film/fow_transcript.html

19. Dowty, *Israel/Palestine,* 63.

20. Dowty, *Israel/Palestine,* 75.

21. Fawaz Turki, *The Disinherited: Journal of a Palestinian Exile* (New York: Monthly Review Press, 1972), 29.

22. Stanley Wolpert, *A New History of India,* 7th ed. (New York: Oxford University Press, 2004), 309.

23. Ibid., 358.

CHAPTER 4

1. See the account in William R. Keylor, *The Twentieth-Century World: An International History,* 4th ed. (New York: Oxford University Press, 2001), 270–71.

2. Ibid.

3. The countries were Belgium, Canada, Columbia, Ethiopia, France, Greece, Luxembourg, the Netherlands, New Zealand, the Philippines, South Africa, South Korea, Thailand, Turkey, and the United States. These countries sent medical units and medical assistance: Denmark, India, Iran, Italy, Norway, and Sweden.

4. Fikru Gebrekidan, "Review of Elkins, Caroline, *Imperial Reckoning: The Untold Story of Britain's Gulag in Kenya,*" H-Africa, H-Net Reviews, April 2006, http://www.h-net.org/reviews/showrev.php?id=11639.

5. Koigi Wa Wamwere, *I Refuse to Die, My Journey for Freedom* (New York: Seven Stories Press, 2003), 99–100.

6. Joel Foreman, "Mau Mau's American Career, 1952–1957," in *The Other Fifties: Interrogating Midcentury American Icons,* ed. Joel Foreman (Urbana: University of Illinois Press, 1997), 78–102.

7. "Caroline Elkins: The Untold Story of Britain's Gulag in Kenya," History News Network, July 3, 2006, 1. https://historynewsnetwork.org/article/30783.

8. Gebrekidan, "Review," 2; "Mau Mau Uprising: Bloody History of Kenya Conflict" *BBC News,* April 7, 2011, 4, https://www.bbc.com/news/uk-12997138.

9. "Caroline Elkins," 1.

10. The Popular Democratic Front garnered only 31 percent of the vote while the Christian Democracy Party gained the most support (48 percent) that they won in any of its elections from 1944 until its demise in 1994.

11. Quoted in Gina Stepp, "When Terror Reigns," *Society and Culture,* Summer 2016, www.vision.org/world-problems-history-of-violence-what-is-terrorism-4748.

12. Frantz Fanon, *The Wretched of the Earth,* trans. Constance Farrington (New York: Grove Press, 1963), 13.

13. Josephine Baker, "Speech at the March on Washington," BlackPast, November 28, 1963 http://www.blackpast.org/1963-josephine-baker-speech-march-washington.

14. Nancy L. Clark and William H. Worger, *South Africa—The Rise and Fall of Apartheid* (Upper Saddle River, NJ: Pearson, 2004), 48–52.

15. UNESCO, "Statistics on Radio and Television, 1950–1960," http://unesdoc.unesco.org/images/0003/000337/033739eo.pdf.

16. Jack Kerouac, *On the Road* (New York: Viking Press, 1957).

17. Allen Ginsberg, *Howl and Other Poems* (San Francisco, CA: City Lights Bookstore, 1956).

18. William S. Burroughs, *Naked Lunch* (New York: Grove Press, 1959).

19. Allen Ginsberg, *Spontaneous Mind: Selected Interviews, 1958–1996* (New York: Harper, 2001), ix.

20. USHistory.org, "America Rocks and Rolls," US History Online Textbook, accessed may 24, 2021, http://www.ushistory.org/us/53d.asp.

21. The Beatles Ultimate Experience, "Paul McCartney Interview: David Frost 12/27/1967," Beatles Interviews Database, accessed May 24, 2021, www.beatlesinterviews.org/db1967.1227.beatles.html.

22. Ibid.

23. BrainyQuote, "George Harrison Quotes," accessed May 24, 2021, www.brainyquote.com/authors/george-harrison-quotes.

24. David Chiu, "The Real 'Dear Prudence' on Meeting Beatles in India," *Rolling Stone*, September 4, 2015, https://www.rollingstone.com/music/music-news/the-real-dear-prudence-on-meeting-beatles-in-india-74048/.

25. "Closing of the Second Vatican Ecumenical Council: Address of Pope Paul VI to Women, 8 December 1965," Paul VI speeches, Libreria Editrice Vaticana, accessed May 24, 2021, http://www.vatican.va/content/paul-vi/en/speeches/1965/documents/hf_p-vi_spe_19651208_epilogo-concilio-donne.html.

26. The first quotation is from General Secretariat, "The Canonization of Pope John XXIII and Pope John Paul II," United States Conference of Catholic Bishops, accessed May 24, 2021, http://www.usccb.org/about/leadership/holy-see/canonizations-john-xxiii-john-paul-ii.cfm; the second from Laura Smith-Spark, Delia Gallagher, and Ben Wederman, "Sainthood for John Paul II and John XXIII, as Crowds Pack St. Peter's Square," CNN, April 28, 2014, http://www.cnn.com/2014/04/27/world/pope-canonization.

CHAPTER 5

1. "10 Abbie Hoffman's Quotes Missing From Your Life," Odyssey Online Learning, accessed May 24, 2021, https://www.theodysseyonline.com/10-abbie-hoffman-quotes-missing-life.

2. "Top 12 Thought-Provoking Steve Biko Quotes," Shoppe Black, December 19, 2016, shoppeblack.us/2016/12/top-steve-biko-quotes.

3. "Steve Biko. The Man, The Movement, The Martyr," *NewAfrican*, December 12, 2012, http://newafricanmagazine.com/steve-biko-the-man-the-movement-the-martyr/.

4. Simone de Beauvoir, *The Second Sex* (New York: Alfred A. Knopf, 1949), 5–6.

5. Sally Scholz, "Simone de Beauvoir: *The Second Sex*," *Philosophy Now*, 2008, Philosophynow.org/issues/69/The_Second_Sex.

6. Robin Bleiweis, "Quick Facts about the Gender Wage Gap," Center for American Progress, March 24, 2020, 1. The Center for American Progress is an independent, nonpartisan policy institute. It is located at 1333 H Street in Washington, DC, 2005. See also "Gender Pay Gap in the United States" Wikipedia, accessed May 24, 2021, https://en.wikipedia.org/wiki/Gender_pay_gap_in_the_United_States; note especially the outline of the "Statistics" section.

7. See Kristen Ghodsee, "Revisiting the United Nations Decade for Women: Brief Reflections on Feminism, Capitalism, and Cold War Politics in the Early Years of the International Women's Movement," Women's Studies International Forum, December 8, 2009, scholar.harvard.edu/files/kristenghodsee/un_decade_reflections.pdf.

8. Gil Troy, "When Feminists Were Zionists," *The Israel Forever Foundation* (blog), n.d., israelforever.org/interact/blog/when_feminists_were_zionists/.

9. "Gay Liberation Front: *Manifesto*," 1971, revised 1978, http://sourcebooks.fordham.edu/pwh/glf-london.asp.

10. Elisabeth Povoledo, "Pope Francis Condemns 'Genocide' of Armenians," *New York Times*, June 24, 2016.

11. Gary J. Bass, *The Blood Telegram: Nixon, Kissinger, and a Forgotten Genocide* (New York: Vintage, 2014).

12. Truong Nhu Tang, with David Chanoff and Doan Van Toai, *A Viet Cong Memoir* (New York: Vintage, 1985), 209.

13. Michael Hunt, *The World Transformed: 1945 to the Present* (New York: Oxford University Press, 2014), 377.

CHAPTER 6

1. Joshua Quittner, "Entry for Berners-Lee in *Time*," *Time*, March 29, 1999.

2. Tom Warren, "The PC Market Just Had Its First Big Growth in 10 Years: The PC Is Far From Dead," The Verge, January 11, 2021, https://www.theverge.com/2021/1/11/22225356/pc-sales-shipments-2020-growth-idc-canalys-remote-work.

3. Daryl Worthington, "Union Carbide Refuses Bhopal Relief Payments," GoodNews, June 2, 2015, http://www.newhistorian.com/union-carbide-refuses-bhopal-relief-payments/3942.

4. Svetlana Alexievich, "Voices from Chernobyl," *The Paris Review* 172 (Winter 2004).

5. Matthew Schofield, "Ruined Chernobyl Nuclear Plant Will Remain a Threat for 3,000 Years," McClatchy DC, April 2016, http://www.mcclatchydc.com/news/nation-world/world/article73405857.html.

6. E. Cardis et al., "Estimates of the Cancer Burden in Europe from Radioactive Fall-out from the Chernobyl Accident," *International Journal of Cancer* 119, no. 6 (2006): 1224.

7. History.com Editors, "Exxon Valdez Oil Spill," History.com, March 23, 2021, http://www.history.com/topics/1980s/exxon-valdez-oil-spill.

8. Report of the World Commission on Environment and Development, *Our Common Future*, n.d., http://www.un-documents.net/our-common-future.pdf.

9. See Joost R. Hiltenmann, *A Poisonous Affair America, Iraq and the Gassing of Halabja* (Washington, DC: Lawfare Institute in Cooperation with Brookings Review, September 17, 2013).

10. This quotation and the material in this paragraph come from Shane Harris and Matthew M. Aid, "Exclusive: CIA Files Prove America Helped Saddam as He Gassed Iran," *Foreign Policy*, August 26, 2013, https://foreignpolicy.com/2013/08/26/exclusive-cia-files-prove-america-helped-saddam-as-he-gassed-iran

11. "Anahita Ratebzad," Wikipedia, accessed May 24, 2021, https://en.wikipedia.org/wiki/Anahita_Ratebzad.

12. For a fuller biography of Ratebzad, see Robert Crews, *Afghan Modern: The History of a Global Nation* (Cambridge, MA: Harvard University Press, 2015), chap. 7.

13. Diana Jean Schemo, "Recession-Ravaged Town Grieves for 6 Children," *New York Times*, December 26, 1991, https://www.nytimes.com/1991/12/26/nyregion/recession-ravaged-town-grieves-for-6-children.html.

14. Padraig O'Malley, *Shades of Difference: Mac Maharaj and the Struggle for South Africa* (New York: Penguin, 2008); Padraig O'Malley, "The Heart of Hope: South Africa's Transition from Apartheid to Democracy," Centre of Memory and Dialogue, Nelson Mandela Foundation, accessed June 2, 2021, https://omalley.nelsonmandela.org/omalley/.

15. Botha made an apartheid pledge even though he was rumored to have moved away from that position. This resource was compiled and authored by Padraig O'Malley. It is the product of almost two decades of research and includes analyses,

chronologies, historical documents, and interviews from the apartheid and post-apartheid eras. For the years 1989 to 1999, O'Malley's work is archived in written transcription and on audio tape at the Robben Island Museum/Mayibuye Archives (University of the Western Cape). His assiduous work of recording the different perspectives and developing attitudes within South Africa during the ten-year period earned Nelson Mandela's highest regard.

CHAPTER 7

1. Pierre Hazan, *Justice in a Time of War* (College Station: Texas A&M University Press, 2004), 77.

2. "Nelson Mandela: Nobel Lecture," The Nobel Prize website, accessed May 24, 2021, https://www.nobelprize.org/prizes/peace/1993/mandela/lecture/.

3. "F.W. de Klerk—Nobel Lecture," The Nobel Prize website, accessed May 24, 2021, https://www.nobelprize.org/prizes/peace/1993/klerk/26129-f-w-de-klerk-nobel-lecture-1993/.

4. Quoted in Reuters, "Factbox: Quotations about Nelson Mandela," *Chicago Tribune*, December 5, 2013.

5. "Yitzhak Rabin: Nobel Lecture," The Nobel Prize website, accessed May 24, 2021, https://www.nobelprize.org/prizes/peace/1994/rabin/lecture/. I have added italics.

6. This analysis comes from Ivo H. Daalder, "Decision to Intervene: How the War Ended in Bosnia," Brookings Institution, December 1, 1998, https://www.brookings.edu/articles/decision-to-intervene-how-the-war-in-bosnia-ended/, and from "Boutros Boutros-Ghali, UN Secretary-General Who Clashed with the U.S. Dies at 93," *Washington Post*, February 16, 2016, https://www.washingtonpost.com/world/boutros-boutros-ghali-un-secretary-general-who-clashed-with-us-dies-at-93/2016/02/16/8b727bb8-d4c1-11e5-be55-2cc3c1e4b76b_story.html.

7. The quotations and detail of these paragraphs come primarily from two sources. See "The Fall of Srebrenica and the Failure of UN Peacekeeping: Bosnia and Herzegovina," *Human Rights Watch* (hereafter, HRW) 7, no. 13 (October 1995), https://www.hrw.org/sites/default/files/reports/bosnia1095web.pdf and Florence Hartmann and Ed Vulliamy, "How Britain and the US Decided to Abandon Srebrenica to Its Fate," *The Guardian*, July 4, 2015, https://www.theguardian.com/world/2015/jul/04/how-britain-and-us-abandoned-srebrenica-massacre-1995.

8. Section of HRW Report: "Offensive against the U.N.-Designated 'Safe Area' of Srebrenica." See also Robert Block, "UN Left 8,000 to Die in Bosnia," *Independent*, October 30, 1995 https://www.independent.co.uk/news/un-left-8-000-die-bosnia-1580101.html.

9. UN British commander lieutenant-general Rupert Smith (at Sarajevo) to the Dutch commander at Srebrenica: "It is too early and not worth the risk." See Block, "UN Left 8,000." See also: "Conference on International Decision Making in the Age of Genocide: Srebrenica 1993–1995," Session 3: The Fall of Srebrenica June 28–July 1, 2015, The Hague Institute for Global Justice, edited transcript, 3–9. Attended by UN and NATO leaders, civilian and military figures who participated in the early July 1995 Srebrenica Crisis.

10. Barbara Crossette, "UN Details Its Failure to Stop '95 Bosnia Massacre," *New York Times*, November 16, 1999, http://www.nytimes.com/1999/11/16/world/un-details-its-failure-to-stop-95-bosnia-massacre.html.

11. Taken from the script of the *Frontline* television program, "The Forgotten Angel of Rwanda," December 3, 2009—a celebration of the life of Mbaye Diagne.

12. Information taken from "Mbaye Diagne," Wikipedia, accessed May 23, 2021, https://en.wikipedia.org/wiki/Mbaye_Diagne, and from Mark Doyle, "A Good Man in Rwanda," *BBC News*, 2014, http://www.bbc.com/news/special/2014/newsspec_6954/index.htm.

13. Terry J. Allen, "Romeo Dallaire: The Man Who Tried to Stop Rwanda's Slaughter," *Amnesty International Magazine*, n.d., http://www.terryjallen.com/journo-subP/dallaire.htm.

14. Stephane Levesque, *Thinking Historically: Educating Students for the Twenty-First Century* (Toronto: University of Toronto Press, 2008), 41.

15. Karina Marlow, "15 Years On, Cathy Freeman's Olympic Gold Still a Potent Symbol of Reconciliation," National Indigenous Television (NITV), December 16, 2015.

16. Peruvian Mario Vargas Llosa, Nobel Prize Lecture, December 10, 2010, https://www.nobelprize.org/prizes/literature/2010/vargas_llosa/speech/.

17. Niall Ferguson, *The War of the World: Twentieth-Century Conflict and the Descent of the West* (New York: Penguin Books, 2006), xxxiv, 649, and 653–54.

18. "UN Human Rights High Commissioneer Zeid Ra'ad al-Hussein Points to Textbook Example of Ethnic Cleansing," *UN News*, September 11, 2017. Specifically he pointed to the flight of some three hundred thousand Rohingha.

19. Mary Dejevsky, "The Principles that Made Aung San Suu Kyi an Icon Are What Undid Her," *The Guardian*, August 28, 2018.

20. Michelle Boorstein, "Holocaust Museum Rescinds Award to Nobel Winner Aung San Suu Kyi," *Washington Post*, March 7, 2018, https://www.washingtonpost.com/news/acts-of-faith/wp/2018/03/07/holocaust-museum-rescinds-elie-weisel-award-to-nobel-winner-san-suu-kyi/.

21. "Amnesty International Withdraws Human Rights Award from Aung San Suu Kyi," Amnesty International, November 12, 2018, https://www.amnesty.org/en/latest/news/2018/11/amnesty-withdraws-award-from-aung-san-suu-kyi/.

22. "Aung San Suu Kyi: The Democracy Icon Who Fell from Grace," *BBC News*, September 13, 2018, https://www.bbc.com/news/world-asia-pacific-11685977.

23. The quotations in this paragraph come from Dejevsky, "Principles."

Further Reading

GENERAL WORKS

Bordo, Michael D., Alan M. Taylor, and Jeffrey G. Williamson, eds. *Globalization in Historical Perspective*. Chicago: University of Chicago Press, 2003.

Glover, Jonathan. *Humanity: A Moral History of the Twentieth Century*. New Haven, CT: Yale University Press, 2000.

Howard, Michael, and Wm. Roger Louis, eds. *The Oxford History of the Twentieth Century*. New York: Oxford University Press, 1998.

Winter, Jay, and Emmanuel Sivan, eds. *War and Remembrance in the Twentieth Century*. Cambridge: Cambridge University Press, 1999.

WORLD WAR I

Barry, John, *The Great Influenza: The Epic Story of the Deadliest Plague in History*. New York: Penguin, 2004.

Chickering, Roger. *Imperial Germany and the Great War, 1914–1918*. Cambridge: Cambridge University Press, 1999.

Fussell, Paul. *The Great War and Modern Memory*. New York: Oxford University Press, 1975.

Hibberd, Dominic. *Wilfred Owen: A New Biography*. Chicago: Ivan R. Dee, 2003.

Horne, John, ed. *State, Society, and Mobilization during the First World War*. Cambridge: Cambridge University Press, 1997.

Keegan, John. *The First World War*. New York: Penguin Random House, 1998.

Suny, Ronald Grigor. *"'They Can Live in the Desert but Nowhere Else": A History of the Armenian Genocide*. Princeton, NJ: Princeton University Press, 2015.

BETWEEN THE WARS

Baker, Jean-Claude, and Chris Chase. *Josephine: The Hungry Heart*. New York: Cooper Square Press, 2001.

Fitzpatrick, Sheila. *Everyday Stalinism: Ordinary Life in Extraordinary Times: Soviet Russia in the 1930s*. Oxford: Oxford University Press, 2000.

Gibson, Ian. *Federico Garcia Lorca*. New York: Pantheon Books, 1989.

Lu Hsun [Xun]. *Selected Stories*. Translated by Yang Hsien-yi and Glays Yang. New York: W. W. Norton, 2003.

Moser, John. *The Global Great Depression and the Coming of World War II*. Abingdon-on-Thames, UK: Routledge, 2015.

Weitz, Eric, D. *Weimar Germany: Promise and Tragedy*. Princeton, NJ: Princeton University Press, 2013.

WORLD WAR II

Dower, John. *War without Mercy: Race and Power in the Pacific War*. New York: Pantheon, 1987.

Hogan, Michael, ed. *Hiroshima in History and Memory*. Cambridge: Cambridge University Press, 1996.

Kershaw, Ian. *Hitler, the Germans, and the Final Solution*. New Haven, CT: Yale University Press, 2009.

Lapierre, Dominique, and Larry Collins. *Freedom at Midnight*. New York: HarperCollins, 1975.

Schoppa, R. Keith. *In a Sea of Bitterness: Refugees during the Sino-Japanese War*. Cambridge, MA: Harvard University Press, 2011.

Shavit, Ari. *My Promised Land: The Triumph and Tragedy of Israel*. New York: Spiegel and Grau, 2015.

Snyder, Timothy. *Bloodlands: Europe between Hitler and Stalin*. New York: Basic Books, 2010.

THE AFTERMATH OF WORLD WAR II

Dobbs, Michael. *One Minute to Midnight: Kennedy, Khrushchev, and Castro on the Brink of Nuclear War*. New York: Knopf, 2008.

Kerouac, Jack. *On the Road*. New York: Penguin, 1999.

Logevall, Fredrik. *Embers of War: The Fall of an Empire and the Making of America's Vietnam*. New York: Random House, 2012.

Stueck, William. *Rethinking the Korean War: A New Diplomatic and Strategic History*. Princeton, NJ: Princeton University Press, 2004.

Westad, Odd Arne. *The Global Cold War*. Cambridge: Cambridge University Press, 2007.

THE WORLD TRANSFORMED

Adamczyk, Amy. *Cross-National Public Opinion about Homosexuality: Examining Attitudes across the Globe*. Chicago: University of Chicago Press, 2017.

Bass, Gary J. *The Blood Telegram: Nixon, Kissinger, and a Forgotten Genocide*. New York: Vintage, 2014.

Etcheson, Craig. *After the Killing Fields: Lessons from the Cambodian Genocide*. Lubbock: Texas Tech University Press, 2006.

Luthi, Lorenz. *The Sino-Soviet Split: Cold War in the Communist World*. Princeton, NJ: Princeton University Press, 2008.

Ma Bo. *Blood Red Sunset: A Memoir of the Cultural Revolution*. New York: Penguin, 1996.

Woods, Donald. *Biko*. New York: Paddington Press, 1978.

THE WORLD AND THE END OF THE COLD WAR

Berners-Lee, Tim. *Weaving the Web: The Original Design and Ultimate Destiny of the World Wide Web*. New York: Harper, 2000.

Kotkin, Stephen. *Armageddon Averted: The Soviet Collapse, 1970–2000*. Oxford: Oxford University Press, 2001.

Monette, Paul. *Borrowed Time: An AIDS Memoir*. New York: Harcourt, 1998.

Siani-Davies, Peter. *The Romanian Revolution of December 1989*. Ithaca, NY: Cornell University Press, 2005.

Tomsen, Peter. *The Wars of Afghanistan: Messianic Terrorism, Tribal Conflicts, and the Failure of Great Powers*. New York: Public Affairs, 2013.

Waldmeir, Patti. *Anatomy of a Miracle: The End of Apartheid and the Birth of the New South Africa*. New York: W. W. Norton, 1997.

THE WORLD AND THE AGE OF GENOCIDES

Dallaire, Romeo. *Shake Hands with the Devil: The Failure of Humanity in Rwanda.* Boston: Da Capo Press, 2004.

Hoffman, Bruce. *Inside Terrorism.* New York: Columbia University Press, 2006.

Macek, Ivana. *Sarajevo under Siege: Anthropology in Wartime. The Ethnology of Political Violence.* Philadelphia: University of Pennsylvania Press, 2011.

Power, Samantha, *"A Problem from Hell": America and the Age of Genocide.* New York: Basic Books, 2002.

Shehadeh, Raja. *Palestinian Walks: Forays into a Vanishing Landscape.* New York: Scribner, 2007.

Websites

1917: Digital Resources on the Russian Revolution

1917resources.aseees.hcommons.org/

Texts, images, video, film, and audio related to the Russian Revolution.

The British Library: World War I

www.bl.uk/world-war-one

An extensive database on World War I, with more than five hundred sources—articles, primary sources, videos, and teaching resources—from across Europe.

China Academic Journals and China Core Newspapers Database—Library of Congress

www.loc.gov/rr/asian/ChineseDB2.html

China National Knowledge Infrastructure (CNKI) databases includes more than ten thousand Chinese academic journals and more than six hundred Chinese newspapers. China Core Newspapers Full-Text Database (CCND) collects academic and informative documents from core newspapers in China since 2000 and is updated continuously.

Chinese Electronic Resources—Library of Congress

www.loc.gov/rr/asian/ChineseDB2.html

This hub has access to a plethora of online resources concerning China. The "Asian Reading Room" includes, but is not limited to, the Database for the History of Contemporary Chinese Political Movements, the *Central Daily News* archives, the *People's Daily*, and the Foreign Office files of China.

Cold War International History Project—Wilson Center Digital Archive

digitalarchive.wilsoncenter.org/browse

Digitized documents on the Cold War era from the archives of former communist countries.

East View—Current Digest of the Russian Press

dlib.eastview.com/browse/publication/6765

Weekly, selected Russian press materials, translated into English (1949–Present).

Gerald R. Ford Presidential Library and Museum—Vietnam Core Collections

Overview: *www.fordlibrarymuseum.gov/library/guides/core_vietnam.pdf*

Selected documents: *https://www.fordlibrarymuseum.gov/library/exhibits/vietnam/vietdocs.asp*

Vietnam Classification Project: *www.fordlibrarymuseum.gov/library/exhibits/vietnam/vietnam.asp*

Selected declassified documents surrounding the war in Vietnam, Cambodia, and Laos, especially during the Nixon and Ford administrations.

Harvard Project on the Soviet Social System, Digital Collection: Interviews and Manuals, 1950–1953

hollisarchives.lib.harvard.edu/repositories/21/resources/6409

A collection of transcripts of interviews conducted with Soviet émigrés to West Germany, Austria, and the United States.

History of Science Research Guides—Smithsonian Libraries

library.si.edu/libraries/dibner-library-history-science-and-technology/researchguide

A comprehensive list of resources related to the history of STEM disciplines.

Korean Electronic Resources—Library of Congress

www.loc.gov/rr/asian/ekorea.html

Access to various Korean research databases such as Bookrail and e-Korean Studies.

Korean Social Science Data Archive

www.kossda.or.kr/eng/

A nonprofit organization with expertise in the acquisition, preservation, and dissemination of Korean social science data and literature.

The Long 19th Amendment Project

long19.radcliffe.harvard.edu/about/

A joint project of the Andrew W. Mellon Foundation and Harvard's Radcliffe Institute for Advanced Study. An open-access digital portal that provides interdisciplinary, transnational scholarship and teaching around the history of gender and voting rights in the United States.

National Archives (US): Vietnam War

www.archives.gov/research/vietnam-war

Photographs, textual and electronic records, exhibits, and other educational resources related to the US experience in the Vietnam conflict.

National Library of Medicine Digital Collections

collections.nlm.nih.gov/

Digitized biomedical books, still images, and videos.

Suffrage School—The Radcliffe Institute for Advanced Study

www.radcliffe.harvard.edu/suffrage-school

Interactive lessons and digital teaching modules related to women's suffrage and the women's movement for equality.

Index

For the benefit of digital users, indexed terms that span two pages (e.g., 52–53) may, on occasion, appear on only one of those pages.

genocides (*cont.*)
  Jews by Germans (1933–45) 55–59
  Rwanda (1972) 101–2
  Rwanda (April–July 1994) 139
  Yugoslavia (1991–99) 134–35
German construction of "white appropriate"
    identity for tribal peoples 10
Germany cultural genocide in Namibia 5–6
German empire, dissolution after World
    War I 29
German-Herero War (January–August
    1904) 2, 8–10
German land fraud
  deceit and cheating 5, 6–7
  greed 5, 7
German-Nama War (October 1904–
    November 1905) 7–8
German war debts to the US, paid
    (2010) 47
Germany, opening the war
  German East Africa 23–24
  role of porters 24
  Southwest Africa 23
  West Africa 22–23
global depression prices 46–47
globalization 11–12
  first world age of 13–15
  foe of individualism 10–11
  foe of nationalism 142–43
  institutional steps (trade and politics) 69–70
  origins of 11
globalization and nationalism, as interpreted
    by Mario Vargas Llosa (1936–) 142–43
Gordimer, Nadine (1923–2014) 131–32
"Great War of Africa" (1998–2003) 140–41
Guernica 51–52

Herero land practices 6–7
Hitler, Adolph (1899–1945) 41–42, 47, 54,
    55, 56–57, 58–59

individual identities, definition and insta-
    bility of 1–2
individual and local allegiance 10–11
international troops to western front
  Vietnamese and Chinese, 24–25
  Indian 27f, 62
  other: Ottoman forces, Australians,
    Canadians, West Africans (Algeria,
    Senegal, and Morocco) 24–25.

Japan
  capture of German territories in China
    and Pacific (August 1918) 22

preparing for World War II 42–45
entering the war 62
ending the war 63

Jewish "Final Solution" 58–59

Karadzik, Radovan (1945–) 137–38
Kariko, Samuel 9
Kenyan Mau Mau uprising 80–82
Korean War (1950–53) 78
Kovel 59

lebensraum (living space) 54
Lettow-Vorbeck, Paul von
    (1870–1964) 23–24
Leutwein, Theodor (1849–1921) 5, 6, 8
Luderitz 9
Lu Xun (1881–1936) 38

Malayan independence 100–1
Malayan insurgency 79–80
Mandela, Nelson (1918–2013) 86, 94, 127–
    28, 129, 130–32
Meitner, Lisa (1878–1968) 57–58
Mendes, Chico (1944–1988) 119
Milosevic, Slobodan (1941–2006) 135, 138
minorities, 98–99
Mladic, Ratko (1942–) 136–38
Mungunda, Hosea 5
music 89–91
Mussolini, Benito (1883–1945) 36, 40–41

Namibian camp prisoners' death rates 9
Namibian fight against German imperialism
    (1885–1915) 3
nation-state and national allegiance as
    political-social-cultural unit 11
natural industrial disasters (1980s)
  Bhopal, India (gas leak) (December 2–3,
    1984) 115
  Chernobyl, Ukraine (nuclear accident)
    (April 26, 1986). *See* Chernobyl nuclear
    disaster
  Exxon Valdez oil spill (March 24,
    1989) 117–19

OPEC (1971–72) 106–7
Oslo Accords (September 1993), 133–34
Ottoman Empire, dissolution after World
    War I 29
Owens, Wilfred (1895–1918) 28
  "Dulcet et Decorum Est" 27–28
  "1914" as inauguration of the coming
    of war 22

The
New
Oxford
World
History

The New Oxford World History provides a comprehensive, synthetic treatment of the "new world history" from chronological, thematic, and geographical perspectives, allowing readers to access the world's complex history from a variety of conceptual, narrative, and analytical viewpoints as it fits their interests.

R. Keith Schoppa is Professor Emeritus of history at Loyola University Maryland, where he served as the Doehler Chair in Asian History from 1998 to 2014. His books include *In a Sea of Bitterness* and *Blood Road: The Mystery of Shen Dingyi in Revolutionary China*, which won the 1997 Association for Asian Studies' Levenson Award.

The
New
Oxford
World
History

CHRONOLOGICAL VOLUMES
The World from 4000 to 1000 BCE
The World from 1000 BCE to 300/500 CE
The World from 300 to 1000 CE
The World from 1000 to 1500
The World from 1450 to 1700
The World in the Eighteenth Century
The World in the Nineteenth Century
The World in the Twentieth Century

THEMATIC AND TOPICAL VOLUMES
The City: A World History
Democracy: A World History
Empires: A World History
The Family: A World History
Race: A World History
Technology: A World History

GEOGRAPHICAL VOLUMES
Central Asia in World History
China in World History
Japan in World History
Russia in World History
The Silk Road in World History
South Africa in World History
South Asia in World History
Southeast Asia in World History
Trans-Saharan Africa in World History